LifeChange

S E R I E S

A NavPress Bible study on the book of

JAMES

NAVPRESS

A MINISTRY OF THE NAVIGATORS
P.O. BOX 35001, COLORADO SPRINGS, COLORADO 80935

The Navigators is an international Christian organization. Jesus Christ gave His followers the Great Commission to go and make disciples (Matthew 28:19). The aim of The Navigators is to help fulfill that commission by multiplying laborers for Christ in every nation.

NavPress is the publishing ministry of The Navigators. NavPress publications are tools to help Christians grow. Although publications alone cannot make disciples or change lives, they can help believers learn biblical discipleship, and apply what they learn to their lives and ministries.

Printed in the United States of America

12 13 14 15 16 17 18 19 20/99 98 97 96 95

CONTENTS

ACKNOWLEDGMENTS

This LIFECHANGE study has been produced through the coordinated efforts of a team of Navigator Bible study developers and NavPress editorial staff, along with a nationwide network of fieldtesters.

SERIES EDITOR: KAREN HINCKLEY

HOW TO USE THIS STUDY

Objectives

Most guides in the LIFECHANGE series of Bible studies cover one book of the Bible. Although the LIFECHANGE guides vary with the books they explore, they share some common goals:

    1. To provide you with a firm foundation of understanding and a thirst to return to the book;

    2. To teach you by example how to study a book of the Bible without structured guides;

    3. To give you all the historical background, word definitions, and explanatory notes you need, so that your only other reference is the Bible;

    4. To help you grasp the message of the book as a whole;

    5. To teach you how to let God's Word transform you into Christ's image.

    Each lesson in this study is designed to take 60 to 90 minutes to complete on your own. The guide is based on the assumption that you are completing one lesson per week, but if time is limited you can do half a lesson per week or whatever amount allows you to be thorough.

Flexibility

LIFECHANGE guides are flexible, allowing you to adjust the quantity and depth of your study to meet your individual needs. The guide offers many optional questions in addition to the regular numbered questions. The optional questions, which appear in the margins of the study pages, include the following:

    Optional Application. Nearly all application questions are optional; we hope you will do as many as you can without overcommitting yourself.

    For Thought and Discussion. Beginning Bible students should be able to handle these, but even advanced students need to think about them. These questions frequently deal with ethical issues and other biblical principles. They often offer cross-references to spark thought, but the references do not give obvious answers. They are good for group discussions.

For Further Study. These include: a) cross-references that shed light on a topic the book discusses, and b) questions that delve deeper into the passage. You can omit them to shorten a lesson without missing a major point of the passage.

If you are meeting in a group, decide together which optional questions to prepare for each lesson, and how much of the lesson you will cover at the next meeting. Normally, the group leader should make this decision, but you might let each member choose his or her own application questions.

As you grow in your walk with God, you will find the LIFECHANGE guide growing with you—a helpful reference on a topic, a continuing challenge for application, a source of questions for many levels of growth.

Overview and Details

The study begins with an overview of James. The key to interpretation is context—what is the whole passage or book *about*?—and the key to context is purpose—what is the author's *aim* for the whole work? In lesson one you will lay the foundation for your study of James by asking yourself, "Why did the author (and God) write the book? What did they want to accomplish? What is the book about?"

In lessons two through eleven you will analyze successive passages of James in detail. Thinking about how a paragraph fits into the overall goal of the book will help you to see its purpose. Its purpose will help you see its meaning. Frequently reviewing a chart or outline of the book will enable you to make these connections.

In lesson twelve, you will review James, returning to the big picture to see whether your view of it has changed after closer study. Review will also strengthen your grasp of major issues and give you an idea of how you have grown from your study.

Kinds of Questions

Bible study on your own—without a structured guide—follows a progression. First you observe: What does the passage *say*? Then you interpret: What does the passage *mean*? Lastly you apply: How does this truth *affect* my life?

Some of the "how" and "why" questions will take some creative thinking, even prayer, to answer. Some are opinion questions without clearcut right answers; these will lend themselves to discussions and side studies.

Don't let your study become an exercise of knowledge alone. Treat the passage as God's Word, and stay in dialogue with Him as you study. Pray, "Lord, what do You want me to see here?" "Father, why is this true?" "Lord, how does this apply to my life?"

It is important that you write down your answers. The act of writing clarifies your thinking and helps you to remember.

Study Aids

A list of reference materials, including a few notes of explanation to help you make good use of them, begins on page 121. This guide is designed to include enough background to let you interpret with just your Bible and the guide. Still, if you want more information on a subject or want to study a book on your own, try the references listed.

Scripture Versions

Unless otherwise indicated, the Bible quotations in this guide are from the New International Version of the Bible. Other versions cited are the Revised Standard Version (RSV), the New American Standard Bible (NASB), and the King James Version (KJV).

Use any translation you like for study, preferably more than one. A paraphrase such as The Living Bible is not accurate enough for study, but it can be helpful for comparison or devotional reading.

Memorizing and Meditating

A psalmist wrote, "I have hidden your word in my heart that I might not sin against you" (Psalm 119:11). If you write down a verse or passage that challenges or encourages you, and reflect on it often for a week or more, you will find it beginning to affect your motives and actions. We forget quickly what we read once; we remember what we ponder.

When you find a significant verse or passage, you might copy it onto a card to keep with you. Set aside five minutes during each day just to think about what the passage might mean in your life. Recite it over to yourself, exploring its meaning. Then, return to your passage as often as you can during your day, for a brief review. You will soon find it coming to mind spontaneously.

For Group Study

A group of four to ten people allows the richest discussions, but you can adapt this guide for other sized groups. It will suit a wide range of group types, such as home Bible studies, growth groups, youth groups, and businessmen's studies. Both new and experienced Bible students, and new and mature Christians, will benefit from the guide. You can omit or leave for later years any questions you find too easy or too hard.

The guide is intended to lead a group through one lesson per week. However, feel free to split lessons if you want to discuss them more thoroughly. Or, omit some questions in a lesson if preparation or discussion time is limited. You can always return to this guide for personal study later. You will be able to discuss only a few questions at length, so choose some for discussion and others for background. Make time at each discussion for members to ask about anything they didn't understand.

Each lesson in the guide ends with a section called "For the group." These sections give advice on how to focus a discussion, how you might apply the lesson in your group, how you might shorten a lesson, and so on. The group leader should read each "For the group" at least a week ahead so that he or she can tell the group how to prepare for the next lesson.

Each member should prepare for a meeting by writing answers for all of the background and discussion questions to be covered. If the group decides not to take an hour per week for private preparation, then expect to take at least two meetings per lesson to work through the questions. Application will be very difficult, however, without private thought and prayer.

Two reasons for studying in a group are accountability and support. When each member commits in front of the rest to seek growth in an area of life, you can pray with one another, listen jointly for God's guidance, help one another to resist temptation, assure each other that the other's growth matters to you, use the group to practice spiritual principles, and so on. Pray about one another's commitments and needs at most meetings. Spend the first few minutes of each meeting sharing any results from applications prompted by previous lessons. Then discuss new applications toward the end of the meeting. Follow such sharing with prayer for these and other needs.

If you write down each other's applications and prayer requests, you are more likely to remember to pray for them during the week, ask about them at the next meeting, and notice answered prayers. You might want to get a notebook for prayer requests and discussion notes.

Notes taken during discussion will help you to remember, follow up on ideas, stay on the subject, and clarify a total view of an issue. But don't let note-taking keep you from participating. Some groups choose one member at each meeting to take notes. Then someone copies the notes and distributes them at the next meeting. Rotating these tasks can help include people. Some groups have someone take notes on a large pad of paper or erasable marker board (preformed shower wallboard works well), so that everyone can see what has been recorded.

Page 124 lists some good sources of counsel for leading group studies. The *Small Group Letter*, published by NavPress, is unique, offering insights from experienced leaders every other month.

INTRODUCTION

James the Just

When the first Christian evangelists proclaimed that people could enter the Kingdom of God simply by believing in Jesus as Lord and Christ, a lot of people accepted the offer. Inevitably, few became spiritual giants overnight. The Apostle Paul wrote many letters to solve problems and amend errors in the churches he founded. And someone who calls himself merely "James, a servant of God and of the Lord Jesus Christ" (1:1) wrote a message to correct a distortion of the gospel: the idea that spiritual rebirth meant we could remain babies forever.

The Lord's brother

James (the English equivalent of *Iakobos* or Jacob) was a common Jewish name; in fact, two of Jesus' twelve apostles were named James (Matthew 10:2-4). However, James the son of Zebedee died too early to have written this letter (44 AD, Acts 12:2), and little is known about James the son of Alphaeus. Tradition attributes the biblical letter to the man Paul calls "James, the Lord's brother" (Galatians 1:19).[1]

James was probably the eldest of the four brothers named in Mark 6:3.[2] While Jesus was wandering through Galilee and Judea proclaiming the Kingdom of God, James and the rest of His family thought He was a bit crazy (Mark 3:20-21, John 7:5). But when Jesus appeared to James after the Resurrection, James finally understood his brother (1 Corinthians 15:7). He became a leader of the church in Jerusalem (Acts 1:14, 15:12-21, 21:17-19)— indeed Paul called him one of the "pillars" of the church (Galatians 2:9). It was James and Peter whom Paul visited three years after his conversion (Galatians 1:18-19), James to whom Peter sent word of his miraculous escape from prison (Acts 12:17), and James whose judgment regarding the Gentiles was accepted by the whole Jerusalem council (Acts 15:13-29).

James was known as "the Just" or "the Righteous" by the people of Jerusalem, both Christian and nonChristian. The fourth-century Christian historian Eusebius said that this was because James was scrupulous about observing the Jewish Law, and Eusebius recorded several legends about James's piety and asceticism. However, the Jewish historian Josephus wrote in 93 AD that James was stoned by the Jews in 62 AD on a charge of violating the Law.[3] There is no evidence that James agreed with the Jewish Christians who said Gentiles could not be saved unless they kept the Jewish Law (Acts 15:1). He did apparently try to make Christianity more appealing to Jews by encouraging Jewish Christians to keep the Law and to avoid eating with Gentiles (Acts 21:17-24, Galatians 2:11-13). Still, James was not claiming that the Law was necessary for salvation, and he did not want to hinder the evangelism of Gentiles (Acts 15:19). James was eager to effect a compromise between Jews and Gentiles on "matters of secondary importance"[4]—cultural things like what to eat (Acts 15:20). However, he was unswervingly opposed to compromise with pagan moral values (Acts 15:20, James 1:21).

A strawy epistle?

In Martin Luther's version of the New Testament published in 1522, he put the books of Hebrews, James, Jude, and Revelation at the end as a supplement rather than in their usual places, and he omitted them from the table of contents. He explained why in his introduction:

> In fine, Saint John's Gospel and his first Epistle, Saint Paul's Epistles, especially those to the Romans, Galatians, Ephesians, and Saint Peter's first Epistle,— these are the books which show thee Christ, and teach thee everything that is needful and blessed for thee to know even though thou never see or hear any other book or doctrine. Therefore is Saint James's Epistle a right strawy Epistle in comparison with them, for it has no gospel character to it.[5]

Luther devalued James because he thought James was responding against Paul's doctrine of justification by faith apart from works. Also, the epistle barely mentions Jesus at all, and never His death and resurrection. In fact, the conflict between Paul and James is only apparent. James shows no sign of ever having read Paul's letters to the Romans or Galatians. He uses words like "justification," "faith," and "works" differently from Paul, and he never addresses Paul's teachings directly.[6] Paul wrote Romans in about 57 AD, and James died in 62 AD, so it is unlikely that James could have seen a copy of Romans.

Some people think James wrote around 45 AD, before Paul began his missionary travels and before there were many Gentiles in the Church.[7] If this date is correct, then James is the earliest New Testament book and is not a reply to distortions of Paul's writings. Instead, it is an exhortation to live what we believe.

On the other hand, some people date the letter around 55-60 AD.[8] If this is right, then James wrote during a time when Paul's views were being widely discussed, misquoted, and misconstrued. Apparently, there were some people in the Church who thought that justification by grace apart from works meant they could disregard God's moral Law. Even Paul had to fight this distortion (Romans 6:1,15).

The gospel of James

Whichever date we choose between 45 and 60 AD, James's message is the same. His focus is much like Jesus', and he is steeped in Jesus' teachings, especially as recorded in Matthew. The poor inherit the Kingdom (James 2:5; compare Matthew 5:3, Luke 6:20); the persecuted are blessed (James 1:12; compare Matthew 5:10-12); deeds of mercy reflect faith in Jesus (James 1:27, 2:14-17; compare Matthew 7:21, 25:31-46); and so on.[9] James takes faith in Jesus the Christ as a given (James 1:1, 2:1) and does not discuss doctrines about Christ. This is natural for someone who grew up with Jesus and is writing to people who have already put faith in Christ. D. A. Hayes concludes, "James says less about the Master than any other writer in the New Testament, but his speech is more like that of the Master than the speech of any of them."[10]

James's faith is still very Jewish, as Jesus' was. While Paul bases his teaching on who Christ is and who we are in Christ, James draws his from who God is and who we are as God's creatures (1:13,16-18; 1:27; 2:5; 3:9; 4:4,6,12,14; 5:4). Paul rhapsodizes on our mystical union with Christ in His death and resurrection, and only later gets practical. James goes straight to the practical: here is how to live in light of the gospel. Paul appears most concerned to explain the gospel to people who don't fully understand it. James seems to think his readers basically know and believe the gospel, but they don't understand its implications for living. God wants more than justified infants. He wants mature daughters and sons. Faith is foundational, but it must be genuine, proven faith, evident to the world.

Far from being a "strawy" epistle, James's letter offers us a vigorous, vital view of Christian faith—a call to tested, mature faith to which Peter, Paul, and Jesus Himself could have said, "Amen."

1. Those who are interested in the debate over who wrote the epistle of James should consult some of the commentaries listed on page 121.
2. When the Church began to put a greater value on celibacy, especially Mary's virginity, it was suggested that the brothers were sons of Joseph by a previous marriage or cousins of Jesus (the word "brother" can have this sense in Greek and Hebrew). Modern Protestant commentators generally think the brothers were sons of Joseph and Mary after Jesus' birth. For a fuller explanation, see R. V. G. Tasker, *The General Epistle of James* (Grand Rapids, Michigan: William B. Eerdmans Publishing Company, 1956), pages 22-24.
3. Flavius Josephus, *Antiquities*, in the Loeb Classical Library, translated by H. St. James Thackeray (Cambridge: Harvard University Press, 1956), 20.9.1.
4. Tasker, page 26.
5. From the introduction to Martin Luther's New Testament of 1522, as translated by J. H. Ropes. Quoted in Tasker, page 14.
6. For more on why Paul and James seem not to be arguing against each other, see E. M. Sidebottom, *James, Jude, 2 Peter* (Grand Rapids, Michigan: William B. Eerdmans Publishing Company, 1967), pages 16-18.

7. Donald W. Burdick, *The NIV Study Bible,* edited by Kenneth Barker (Grand Rapids, Michigan: Zondervan Corporation, 1985), page 1879; Henry C. Theissen, *Introduction to the New Testament* (Grand Rapids, Michigan: William B. Eerdmans Publishing Company, 1943), page 277.
8. Sidebottom, pages 11-18; Tasker, pages 30-33; Peter H. Davids, *The Epistle of James* (Grand Rapids, Michigan: William B. Eerdmans Publishing Company, 1982), pages 2-22.
9. Sidebottom lists three full pages of parallels between James's letter and Matthew's Gospel in Sidebottom, pages 8-11.
10. D. A. Hayes, "Epistle of James," *The International Standard Bible Encyclopaedia,* Volume 3, edited by James Orr (Grand Rapids, Michigan: William B. Eerdmans Publishing Company, 1956), page 1564.

OVERVIEW

If you are like most people when you receive an important letter, you probably read it straight through first to see what the writer has to say in general. After that, you may go back to examine particular sections more closely. This is just the way to study a biblical letter. In this lesson, you'll take a broad overview of James's epistle to lay the groundwork for detailed study in future lessons.

1. James is an elder of the church in Jerusalem, a man who knew Jesus well during His earthly life and who saw Him after His resurrection. As a Christian in some distant province of the Roman Empire, you have probably never met James. Still, he cares enough about you to send some of the truths he thinks are crucial to Christian life. Read his letter through at one sitting. If possible, read it twice in different translations. Say some of it aloud to hear how it sounds. You may want to keep questions 2 through 6 in mind as your read, but wait until afterward to write answers.

2. What are your first impressions of this book? (For instance, how is it organized—tightly, loosely, with one unifying theme, without connections between topics . . . ? What is James's tone—humorous, harsh, friendly, dry, passionate, humble, arrogant, authoritative? How does he feel about his readers and his topics?)

For Thought and Discussion: Observe James's use of picture words ("mist," "corroded," "fresh water and salt water," etc.). How do these vivid words contribute to his message?

_____

_____

_____

_____

_____

_____

_____

_____

3. Repetition is a clue to the ideas a writer wants to emphasize. What words and ideas does James repeat?

_____

_____

_____

_____

_____

_____

4. Think of a short phrase or sentence that can serve as a title for each section of the letter. (The divisions below are suggestions. Feel free to change them.)

1:1 _____

1:2-18 _____

_____

1:19-27 _____

_____

2:1-13 _____

_____

2:14-26 _____

_____

3:1-12 _____

_____

3:13-18 _____

_____

4:1-10 _____

_____

4:11-12 _____

_____

4:13-17 _____

_____

5:1-6 _____

_____

5:7-12 _____

_____

5:13-20 _____

_____

For Further Study:
Compare James's attitude toward God's Law to the one described in Psalm 119:97-104. What similarities do you see?

5. How would you describe James's purpose(s) for writing this letter? (Is he teaching doctrine, exhorting someone to action, giving warnings or rebukes, telling about himself, offering personal comfort or encouragement . . . ?)

_____

_____

_____

_____

_____

_____

6. Some people find no single theme in this letter, while others do see a theme running through all his words. What phrase or sentence would you use to summarize what James is saying?

_____

_____

_____

_____

Study Skill—Overviews

You will probably find overviews enormously helpful when you study books of the Bible on your own. You can use this lesson as a model for your own overviews. Include the following steps:

1. Read the whole book at least once, preferably at one sitting. (This may be hard with long books.)

2. Jot down your first impressions, such as the author's tone of voice, his attitudes toward his readers and himself, how he organizes his message, and how he presents his message (stories, pictures, instructions, descriptions of people or events, poetry, logical reasoning, etc.).

3. Sketch a broad outline of the book by giving titles to major sections. (You can compare your titles to those in some study Bibles, handbooks, and commentaries.)

4. Write down as many repeated words and ideas as you can find. (Of course, don't bother with words like *the* or *and*).

5. Decide what you think is the author's purpose for writing.

6. State what you think are the themes of the book—the main ideas that the author is trying to get across.

7. If you haven't already read the Introduction on pages 9-12, do so now.

8. After reading the letter and the Introduction, what are some of the questions that you would

like to have answered as you delve more deeply into James's epistle? (Your questions can serve as personal objectives for your study.)

_____

_____

_____

_____

_____

_____

_____

Study Skill—Application

In 1:22 James writes, "Do not merely listen to the word, and so deceive yourselves. Do what it says." In other words, application is an essential part of Bible study. Every lesson of this study contains both "Optional Applications" in the margins and at least one open-ended application question after the interpretation questions. Application will often require some time for thought, prayer, planning, and action. You may want to discuss the passage with someone else to help you decide how to apply it. You'll be looking for specific ways to do what God's Word says.

Some questions to ask yourself are, "What difference should this passage make to my life? How should it make me want to think or act?" At times, you may find it most productive to concentrate on one application, giving it careful thought, prayer, and effort during the week. At other times, you may want to list many implications a passage has for your life, plan to memorize and meditate on the passage during the week, and look for ways to apply it. Choose whatever strategy is most fruitful.

Don't neglect prayer. As John 15:1-5 points out, you can't do what the Word says unless you are living intimately with Christ

(continued on page 18)

(continued from page 17)
and drawing on His power. Go to God for guidance about what to apply and how, for strength to do what He says, for forgiveness when you fail, and for thanksgiving when you succeed.

9. Did your overview of James suggest any areas of your life that you want to work on during this study? If so, jot them down, along with any plans you already have to deal with them. Take each one to God in prayer, asking Him to show you His priorities for your application and to give you His strength to become what He desires. If any of James's words have convicted you, confess your failings to God.

_____

_____

_____

_____

_____

_____

For the group

This "For the group" section and the ones in later lessons are intended to suggest ways of structuring your discussions. Feel free to select what suits your group and ignore the rest. The main goals of this lesson are to get to know James's letter as a whole and the people with whom you are going to study it.

Worship. Some groups like to begin with prayer and/or singing. Some share requests for prayer at the beginning, but leave the actual prayer until after the study. Others prefer just to chat and have refreshments for a while and then move to the study, leaving worship until the end. It is a good idea to start with at least a brief prayer for the Holy Spirit's guidance and some silence to help everyone change focus from the day's business to the Scripture.

Warm-up. The beginning of a new study is a good time to lay a foundation for honest sharing of ideas, to get comfortable with each other, and to encourage a sense of common purpose. One way to establish common ground is to talk about what each group member hopes to get out of your group—out of your study of James, and out of any prayer, singing, sharing, outreach, or anything else you might do together. Why do you want to study the Bible, and James in particular? If you have someone write down each member's hopes and expectations, then you can look back at these goals later to see if they are being met. Allow about fifteen minutes for this discussion so that it does not degenerate into vague chatting.

How to use this study. If the group has never used a LIFECHANGE study guide before, you might take a whole meeting to get acquainted, discuss your goals, and go over the "How to Use This Study" section on pages 5-8. Then you can take a second meeting to discuss the overview. This will assure that everyone understands the study and will give you more time to read all of James and answer the overview questions.

Go over the parts of the "How to Use This Study" section that you think the group should especially notice. For example, point out the optional questions in the margins. These are available as group discussion questions, ideas for application, and suggestions for further study. It is unlikely that anyone will have the time or desire to answer all the optional questions. A person might do one "Optional Application" for any given lesson. You might choose one or two "For Thought and Discussions" for your group discussion, or you might spend all your time on the numbered questions. If someone wants to write answers to the optional questions, suggest that he use a separate notebook. It will also be helpful for discussion notes, prayer requests, answers to prayers, application plans, and so on.

Invite everyone to ask questions about how to use the study guide and how your discussions will go.

Reading. It is often helpful to refresh everyone's memory by reading the passage aloud before discussing the questions. Reading all of James may take some time, but the effort will be rewarded. Have a different person read each chapter, using the tone of voice he or she thinks James would have used. Try to make the letter sound like a living person talking.

First impressions. If members don't understand question 2, ask how James's letter is like and unlike ones they write, or like and unlike a sermon, advice from a father, an essay, one of Paul's letters, and so on. Some aspects of style that you might draw attention to are:

1. picture words ("like a wave of the sea," "like a wild flower," "ships," "a great forest fire," etc.) rather than abstract words (such as "faithless" or "brief");
2. lots of commands and exhortations stated in simple, blunt sentences;
3. a tone of authority;
4. James's affection for his readers ("brothers," "dear brothers").

The character of the author is an important part of understanding a letter. Ask someone to tell what he or she knows about James and the circumstances in which he was probably writing.

Some people dislike to give any attention to the human author of inspired Scripture because this seems to denigrate its divine authority. If necessary, explain that this series takes the view that just as Jesus was fully God and fully Man, so the books of the Bible are eternal messages from the Spirit of God and messages from particular men in particular times and places. Just as Jesus' humanity and divinity are both essential to His mission and nature, so the humanity and divinity of the biblical books are both important. When we discuss James as the writer of this letter, we are in no way denying divine inspiration.

Compare your answers to questions 3 through 6. You might also look together at some outlines of James in study Bibles or commentaries. Remember that there is no one right way to title a passage.

Questions. Give everyone a chance to share questions about the Introduction and the letter. It is good to clear up any confusion as early as possible.

However, don't answer any questions that deal with specific passages. Write those down and let the group answer them when you get to the passages.

Application. If application is new to some group members, you might make up some sample applications together. Choose a paragraph or verse and think of how it is relevant to you and some specific things you could each do about it. Share your answers to question 9. If there is real confusion about application, see the Study Skill on page 40.

Wrap-up. The group leader should have read lesson two and its "For the group" section. At this point, he or she might give a short summary of what members can expect in that lesson and the coming meeting. This is chance to whet everyone's appetite, assign any optional questions, omit any numbered questions, or forewarn members of possible difficulties.

Encourage any members who found the overview especially difficult. Some people are better at seeing the big picture than others. Some are best at analyzing a particular verse or paragraph, while others are strongest at seeing how a passage applies to their lives. Urge members to give thanks for their own and others' strengths, and to give and request help when needed. The group is a place to learn from each other. Later lessons will draw on the gifts of close analyzers as well as overviewers and appliers, practical as well as theoretical thinkers.

Worship. Many groups like to end with singing and/or prayer. This can include songs and prayers that respond to what you've learned in James or prayers for specific needs of group members. Some people are shy about sharing personal needs or praying aloud in groups, especially before they know the other people well. If this is true of your group, then a song and/or some silent prayer, and a short closing prayer spoken by the leader, might be an appropriate end. You could also share requests and pray in pairs.

JAMES 1:1-8

Facing Trials

It is not easy to be a Christian, least of all in Jerusalem, where James lives. Traditional Jews are scandalized at the claim that an executed criminal is the Messiah, and they have killed some Christians and persecuted others. Pagans find their power, incomes, self-esteem, and religious beliefs challenged, and they retaliate with discrimination and outright violence (Acts 7:54-8:3, 12:1-3, 13:44-52, 14:19-22, 16:16-24, 17:5-15, 18:12-17, 19:23-41, 21:27-36). Judea, especially Jerusalem, is seething with fury against the Roman occupiers and all Jews who cooperate with them. Assassins and terrorists are in every crowd. Rome is responding with an iron fist. Within a few years there will be war.

James knows what his people are going through. Besides having to earn their livings, pay taxes, raise their families, and care for their health, they must also reckon with neighbors who think them strange and antisocial for their beliefs and lifestyles. But James faces the same obstacles, and he counsels his brothers and sisters with frank realism.

Read 1:1-8, asking God to speak to you in your circumstances.

Greeting (1:1)

Servant (1:1). This could be either a slave who belongs to his master or a servant who freely

For Thought and Discussion: How is it significant that James calls himself a servant of both God and "the Lord Jesus Christ"?

chooses to work for his master. In the Old Testament, God's servants are His special envoys and representatives, such as Abraham, Moses, David, and the prophets.

Twelve tribes scattered among the nations (1:1). The most literal interpretation would be Jewish Christians among "the dispersion," those Jews who lived outside Palestine. Some think that James is speaking figuratively of all Christians as the true Israel scattered among the unbelieving nations (see 1 Peter 1:1).

God scattered the people of Israel as a punishment for their sins, but He promised through the prophets to regather them and restore the nation. The Jews expected the Messiah to do this, and Jesus said He would return and gather His people into His Kingdom (Mark 13:26-27; John 14:3; 1 Thessalonians 4:16-17). Until then, the citizens of the Kingdom live scattered in the world, facing the tests that prepare us for our future with Him.

The reason for trials (1:2-8)

Trials (1:2,12) . . . *tempted* (1:13-14). The Greek for "trial" and "temptation" is the same. James is trying to help his readers see the distinction between trials that come from outward circumstances and temptations that come from our hearts.

1. How do you normally feel and respond when you have to face a trial?

_____

_____

_____

_____

_____

_____

24

2. How does James tell those scattered in the world to respond to trials (1:2)?

_____

_____

For Further Study:
For examples of biblical people perfected by trials, see Jesus (the gospels and Hebrews 2:10), Abraham (Genesis 12-22), and David (1 Samuel 16:1-2 Samuel 23:7).

> **Study Skill—Tracing Themes in Scripture**
> It is often a great help to trace a theme or topic throughout the Bible, to learn what the whole of Scripture says on the subject. If you can come up with a key word, such as *humility*, then you can use a concordance. With a topic such as trials and sufferings, you might need a topical Bible.

3. Why should we respond like this? What progression of the Christian life does James describe in 1:3-4?

_____

_____

_____

_____

4. What James says in 1:3-4 and similar ideas are repeated over and over in Scripture. Read the following cross-references, and briefly write down what each says about trials and suffering.

Matthew 5:11-12 _____

_____

_____

Romans 5:3-5 _____

_____

_____

Hebrews 2:10 _____

_____

_____

For Thought and Discussion: How is it possible to cultivate joy amid trials? See, for example, Romans 15:3,13; Ephesians 3:14-21; Hebrews 10:19-25.

Hebrews 12:11 _____

_____

_____

1 Peter 1:6-7 _____

_____

_____

5. What can we conclude from all these passages?

_____

_____

_____

_____

_____

6. Suffering is apparently *the* way in which God produces perseverance and maturity in us. Why do you think trials are so effective at this and nothing else is so effective? (*Optional:* See 2 Corinthians 1:8-9, 12:7-10.)

_____

_____

_____

_____

_____

7. What is "perseverance" (1:3)? Look it up in an English dictionary if you can't give a clear definition.

_____

_____

_____

_____

Wisdom (1:5-8)

For Further Study:
a. What does Proverbs 9:10-12 tell you about wisdom? Why must one fear the Lord in order to be truly wise? How can you apply this counsel?

b. Using a concordance, study other references to wisdom in Proverbs.

Study Skill—Repetition

James seems to connect 1:5 to 1:4 by repeating the word *lack*. The mature person lacks nothing that pertains to Christian character (1:4). But some of us may lack some things, such as wisdom (1:5).

As you study other passages and books, watch for repetition that shows a connection between ideas.

For Thought and Discussion: What is the difference between a smart and a wise person?

Wisdom (1:5). "The discipline of applying truth to one's life in the light of experience."[1] Wisdom is meant to be not theoretical and abstract, but practical and personal. It should enable a person to live responsibly and successfully. Yet it is not just the skill of getting ahead and looking out for self, since "success" is defined according to God's values of serving God and others. Proverbs 9:10 says, "The fear of the LORD is the beginning of wisdom."

The discipline of Wisdom had a long tradition in Israel. In the Bible, the books of Proverbs, Job, and Ecclesiastes are books about Wisdom.

---

8. In the middle of discussing trials, James mentions wisdom (1:5). What does wisdom have to do with facing trials? Why should we pray for wisdom, not just perseverance?

_____

_____

_____

_____

_____

_____

For Thought and Discussion: God assures us that if we ask according to His will, He always hears and answers us (1 John 5:14-15). Do you think wisdom is ever contrary to God's will? If so, when? If not, how should this affect our faith when asking for wisdom?

Optional Application: a. Have you ever had to depend on someone who found fault with you when you asked for things? Why is it significant to you personally that God "gives generously to all without finding fault" (1:5)? Meditate on this fact and write down the implications it has for your life. Ask God to help you believe this about Him completely. Ask Him to show you if there is anything in your heart in the way of your believing this.
  b. For cross-references, see Luke 11:5-13, 18:1-8.

9. When we ask for wisdom, it is important that we believe something about God. What must we believe (1:5-8)?

_____

_____

_____

_____

_____

10. Why is it crucial that we believe this with our whole minds and hearts (1:6-8)?

_____

_____

_____

_____

_____

Double-minded (1:8, 4:8). James has a lot to say about doubleness, wavering, inconsistency, facing now one way and now another. In contrast to the person of divided mind and loyalty, we find God, "who does not change like shifting shadows" (1:17). The opposite of double-mindedness is single-mindedness, purity of heart (Matthew 5:8; James 1:27, 3:17, 4:8). Watch for the idea of doubleness versus singleness in James's letter.

Your response

11. Describe one or more of the trials or testings you are currently facing.

_____

_____

_____

_____

_____

_____

12. From 1:2-8, what are some of the attitudes you should have about this trial?

_____

_____

_____

_____

_____

13. How can you cooperate with God in accomplishing the purposes for which He is allowing this trial (1:3-4)? What can you do this week to let God use this situation to make you more mature and like His Son?

_____

_____

_____

_____

_____

14. Is there any other insight from 1:1-8 that you would like to take to heart? If so, what is it?

_____

_____

_____

_____

_____

Optional Application: Ask God for wisdom to deal with your trials as Jesus would have. Make this a persistent prayer this week.

For Further Study: Why is faith essential to receiving answers to prayer (Mark 11:20-24, Hebrews 11:6)?

Optional Application: a. God is single-minded about His goal for your life (1:2-4). What is that goal? How does He plan to achieve it?

b. Are you equally single-minded about reaching this goal? Or do you have some of the traits of a double-minded person (1:6-8)? Pray for single-mindedness.

c. What are you doing and not doing to cooperate with God's plan for your life? Pray about this and ask God for wisdom. Commit yourself to take some action to cooperate with God in achieving your maturity.

29

For Further Study:
What can churches
and fellowships do to
help double-minded,
unstable people
become mature? See
Ephesians 4:7-16.
How could your
church or fellowship
apply this?

15. If you have any questions about 1:1-8 or anything in this lesson, write them here.

_____

_____

_____

_____

For the group

Worship.

Warm-up. People often come to Bible studies with
their minds still churning over the day's events.
Singing and prayer can help people refocus onto
God and His Word. Another method you may find
helpful is to begin with a question that deals with
people's lives and is related to the topic at hand.
Either question 1 or 13 can serve this purpose.

Read aloud. Have someone read 1:1-8.

Summarize. Ask someone to tell briefly what 1:1-8 is
about. This need not be an exhaustive summary,
since it is meant only to keep you from losing sight
of the forest when you examine the trees.

Questions. Touch quickly on observation questions
(such as question 2) and meanings of key words
("What does 'perseverance' mean? What is 'wisdom'?"). Spend more time on thought questions
like questions 5, 6, and 8. You might assign a few
cross-references to each person ahead of time so
that the whole group does not have to search for all
of them.

Don't expect to be able to cover more than one
or two of the optional questions. Choose those that
you think will be interesting and relevant for the
group.

Try to spend about half of your time discussing
how you would like to apply 1:1-8 to yourselves.
Question 14 is an open-ended application question,
while questions 11-13 are more directive. You can
also ask how specific verses are relevant to the
group. The "Optional Applications" do this, and you
can make up your own for any verse.

Worship. Thanking and praising God for what you have studied may help inscribe it on your hearts and move you into greater love for God. For example, thank Him for the trials each of you is facing. Thank Him for testing your faith, and for developing perseverance and maturity in you.

Pray for wisdom and endurance in your trials. Pray specifically for anyone who wants prayer for some trial. Prayer is often a good way to begin as a group to apply what you have studied, since prayer is the foundation of all authentic application.

1. Gordon Fee and Douglas Stuart, *How to Read the Bible for All Its Worth* (Grand Rapids, Michigan: Zondervan Corporation, 1982), page 187.

JAMES 1:9-18

Trial or Temptation?

There is really no break in James's train of thought between 1:8 and 1:9; we divided the section only to keep the lessons at manageable lengths. So, read all of 1:2-18 in preparation for this lesson.

Rich and poor (1:9-11)

Study Skill—Context

It is important to study verses in context, rather than seeing them as isolated statements. In nearly every book, the author is following a train of thought. Each statement is meant to contribute to a larger, whole message.

For example, since 1:2-4 and 1:12-18 are clearly about trials and temptations, it is reasonable to infer that 1:5-8 and 1:9-11 are on the same topic. The context (trials) suggests that James intends praying for wisdom (1:5-8) to be a way of dealing with trials while our faith is being tested. Likewise, the context suggests that James means 1:9-11 to be examples of trials we may face.

It is sometimes harder to trace James's train of thought than it is to follow Paul's logic in his letters. However, try to keep these two questions in mind whenever you study a passage of Scripture:

(continued on page 34)

(continued from page 33)

For Thought and Discussion: Why would a person take pride in a low position? What sort of pride is James talking about?

For Thought and Discussion: How should 1:10-11 affect your attitude toward your career and your possessions?

1. What is the author saying in this passage?
2. Why does he say it here? (That is, what does it have to do with what comes before and after?)

There are certainly times when a writer breaks off abruptly and begins on a totally new subject, but those are the exception. Reading passages like James 1:5-11 in context helps us to see more fully what James is getting at.

1. What is the "high position" in which the brother without wealth should take pride (James 1:9, 2:5)? (*Optional:* See Luke 6:20, Colossians 1:27.)

_____

_____

_____

_____

2. In what "low position" should the rich believer take pride (1:10-11)?

_____

_____

_____

3. How is each person's position potentially a trial that can bring perseverance and maturity?

the humble brother's high position _____

_____

_____

_____

_____

the rich brother's low position _____

_____

34

_____

_____

_____

For Further Study:
What crowns are
given in each of the
following passages,
and who receives
them:
  1 Corinthians 9:25
  1 Thessalonians
    2:19-20
  2 Timothy 4:8
  1 Peter 5:4
  Revelation 2:10

A blessing (1:12)

4. What promises encourage us to have joy (1:2)
   amid trials (1:12)? (*Optional:* See also Matthew
   5:11-12; Hebrews 10:34, 12:2; 1 Peter 1:6-7.)

_____

_____

_____

_____

_____

_____

_____

Crown (1:12). Victorious athletes and military leaders were crowned with garlands of flowers or
wreaths of leaves. A different word was used for
a king's crown. The victory crown for the Christian who perseveres is eternal *life*.

5. Summarize the results of trials that James
   names in 1:1-12 (1:3-4,12) and how we should
   therefore respond to trials (1:2,5-11).

   results _____

   _____

   _____

   _____

   response _____

   _____

Temptation (1:13-18)

James is interested in practical faith, but he knows that the practical must be rooted in true beliefs. When trials come from without, we may be ruined by not understanding God's single-minded, loving purpose to mature us (1:1-12). Likewise, when evil tempts us, we may wrongly believe that God is out to get us or that "the devil made us do it." Once again, godly practice can be grounded only in a true perception of God's nature and our own.

Tempted (1:13-14). Remember that although *temptation*, *trial*, and *testing* all reflect the same Greek word-group, the Bible distinguishes among them. God led Israel into the wilderness to test the people's faith (Exodus 20:20; Deuteronomy 8:2,16), and God also tested Abraham's faith by commanding him to sacrifice his son (Genesis 22:1). The Spirit of God led Jesus into the wilderness to be tempted by Satan (Matthew 4:1). Satan tempted Jesus to evil, but God permitted it for good—as a test and refining of Jesus' faith (Hebrews 2:10,18; 4:15-16; James 1:2-4). Job had the same experience (Job 1:6-2:10, 42:1-6).

6. God is never the source of temptation to evil (1:13). Of what things is He the source (1:5,16-18)?

_____

_____

_____

_____

_____

_____

7. From what you know about God's nature, why is it impossible that God could be responsible for your being tempted to do evil? (*Optional:* See 1 John 1:5, 4:8-10.)

_____

_____

_____

_____

_____

For Thought and Discussion: In 1:14, is James denying that the devil tempts us? Why or why not? (See 4:7-8.)

For Thought and Discussion: Why is it personally important to you that temptations do not come from God?

8. a. What is the real source of temptations to sin (1:14)?

_____

_____

_____

For Thought and Discussion: Why do you think a person would blame God for sending temptations?

b. What is the ultimate result (1:15)?

_____

_____

_____

c. The truth of 1:15 is an unavoidable law, as certain as the law of gravity. Think about the source of life. Why must desiring evil lead to death? (*Optional:* See Isaiah 59:2; 1 John 1:5-7, 5:11-13.)

_____

_____

_____

_____

_____

_____

9. God is the source of "every good and perfect gift" (1:17). What gifts would be helpful in deal-

For Further Study:
What can we do about
many evil desires
(2 Timothy 2:22,
James 4:7-8)?

For Further Study:
See the progression
from desire to sin to
death in Eve's life
(Genesis 3:6-22).

For Further Study:
How did Jesus urge
His disciples to deal
with temptation (Mat-
thew 6:13, 26:41)?
How might this apply
to you?

**For Thought and
Discussion:** Have
you ever had to
depend on someone
who changed like
shifting shadows, so
you could never be
sure what they might
do? Why is it impor-
tant to you that God
isn't like that (1:17)?

ing with one's evil desires? (See, for example,
James 1:5, Luke 11:11-12.)

_____

_____

_____

_____

_____

Notice the two alternate progressions of life that
James has described:

Faith—trials that test it—perseverance—
maturity (1:2-4).
or
Desire—temptation—sin—death (1:14-15).

We can go from tested faith to maturity, or from
indulged desire to death. Each process is a slow,
almost imperceptible series of choices made
daily. Choices lead to habits, and habits set a
character turned either toward or against God.

Father of the heavenly lights (1:17). Literally,
"father of lights." The fact that God is the Crea-
tor of the sun, moon, stars and planets has several implications. They are some of His most
splendid works, glittering examples of the
"good and perfect gift[s]" He sends us. They are
symbols of His truth and moral purity, as John
says, "God is light; in him there is no darkness
at all" (1 John 1:5). Yet they fall short of His
perfection: eclipses and clouds shade their light,
yet in God "is no variation or shadow due to
change" (James 1:17, RSV). Or, as the NIV reads,
God "does not change like shifting shadows"
cast by the heavenly lights.

Firstfruits (1:18). Each year in Israel, the first sheaf
of harvested grain (the firstfruits) was offered to
God as a sign that the whole belonged to Him
and would soon be gathered in (Leviticus
23:9-14). The firstfruits were first in quality as
well as time.

10. What do you think "He chose to give us birth through the word of truth" (1:18) means? (Is James talking about natural birth [Genesis 1:26-27, 2:4-7] or spiritual rebirth [1 Peter 1:23-25]?)

_____

_____

_____

_____

_____

Study Skill—Summarizing and Outlining

If you summarize a passage after you study it, you may find yourself better able to grasp its main point now and remember it later. Try to use one sentence. Your titles on pages 14-15 may be helpful.

The next step toward organizing and remembering a passage is to outline it. Question 4 on page 14 is a broad outline of the whole book; you can add outlines for each passage that are as detailed as you like. You can make an outline as you go along or wait until you have finished the book.

---

11. From 1:1-18, how would you summarize the difference between trials and temptations?

_____

_____

_____

_____

_____

_____

_____

_____

Optional Application: Meditate on God's constancy. How does it affect your attitudes, feelings, and choices?

For Thought and Discussion: Have you ever experienced what James describes in 1:14-15? Think of an example and confess it to God.

For Thought and Discussion: What difference should it make to your life that you are "a kind of firstfruits of all he created" (1:18)?

For Further Study: Begin an outline of James with 1:1-18. Try to show James's train of thought—the connections between each idea and paragraph.

Study Skill—Application

You may find the following steps helpful in planning an application:

1. Record the verse or passage that contains the truth you want to apply to your life. If the passage is short enough, consider copying it word for word, as an aid to memory.

2. State the truth of the passage that impresses you. For instance: *"God is completely dependable, like an unchanging light (1:17). He is absolutely holy and good. He is responsible for the good things in my life, including trials that lead to maturity, but I am responsible for entertaining temptation to sin (1:13-14)."*

3. Describe how you already see this truth at work in your life. For example: *"God has given me physical life, eternal life, and the ability to resist temptation. He enabled me to overcome self-pity during the illness I had several years ago. He enabled me to forgive my parents for the ways they treated me as a child."*

4. Tell how you fall short or want to grow in relation to this truth. (Ask God to help you see yourself clearly.) For example: *"I tend to blame God for my weaknesses because I feel guilty about giving in to my desires. I focus more on my faults and desires than on the good things God gives. In particular, I blame God for the situation at work that makes me often irritable, even at my spouse."*

5. State precisely what you plan to do about having your life changed in this area. Ask God what you can do. Don't forget that transformation depends on His will, power, and timing, not on yours. Diligent prayer should always be part of your application (1:5). For instance: *"I will confess to my spouse the guilt and anger I have been feeling and the wrong ways I have been treating him/her. I will thank God each day this week for all the good gifts He has given me. I will ask Him to help me not to give in to the temptation to lash out at others or to nurse*

(continued on page 41)

(continued from page 40)

anger inside. To accomplish this, I will need to spend at least a half hour in prayer each day, focusing intently on who God is, as described in 1:13-18."

6. Plan a way to remind yourself of what you have decided, such as putting a note on your refrigerator or desk, or asking a friend or relative to remind you. You might also want to ask that person to pray with you about your plans.[1]

12. What one insight from 1:9-18 seems most personally signficant to you right now?

_____

_____

_____

_____

_____

13. How do you see this truth already affecting your life?

_____

_____

_____

_____

_____

14. How do you fall short or need to grow in this area? (Be as specific as possible.)

_____

_____

_____

_____

_____

15. What can you do this week to act on this insight?

_____

_____

_____

_____

_____

_____

16. How can you make sure you remember to do this?

_____

_____

_____

_____

17. If you have any questions about 1:9-18 or this lesson, write them here.

_____

_____

_____

_____

For the group

Warm-up. Ask everyone to think of one temptation he or she has been experiencing recently. Then ask everyone to decide what the source of this temptation seems to be—something inward or something external? Let the group think about this silently for a minute, then move on.

Read aloud and summarize.

Questions. Be sure everyone grasps the two progressions from faith to maturity and from desire to death. Also, be sure each person understands what

James says about God's nature. These truths are foundational to the specific exhortations he gives.

Try to plan at least fifteen minutes to share how each of you plans to apply something in 1:9-18. Discuss your efforts to apply James since your last meeting, and consider whether you might approach application differently. What have you learned about applying Scripture that might help other members?

Worship. Praise the Father of lights for never changing like shadows that cross the sun. Thank Him for choosing to give you birth through the Word of truth, so that you would be a kind of first-fruits of all He created. Praise Him for giving you every good gift and never tempting you to evil. Name aloud some of the gifts He has given you. Thank Him for assuring you of the crown of life if you stand firm.

1. This "Five-point Application" is based on the method in *The 2:7 Series*, Course 4 (Colorado Springs, Colorado: NavPress, 1979), pages 50-51.

LESSON FOUR

JAMES 1:19-27

Doing What You Hear

Now that we are clear that the sources of temptation
to do evil are inside us and that the wisdom and
gifts to resist are available from God, James can
exhort us to use God's good gifts to do what is
right. As you read 1:19-27, ask God to convict you.

Listening and doing (1:19-27)

1. Below, list both the negative and the positive
   admonitions James gives in 1:19-27.

Positive (to do)	Negative (to reject or stop doing)

Optional Application: Do you have a problem with either talkativeness or anger? If so, ask God for wisdom and grace to overcome your failing. Watch for times when you are angry or too talkative this week, and confess them. Keep asking for grace to change.

For Thought and Discussion: a. What part does humility play in our receiving and applying God's Word? Why is it so essential?

b. What inner and outer influences can make it hard sometimes for us to humbly accept God's words (1:21)?

Optional Application: a. What keeps you from being quick to listen?

b. How can you grow better at listening? How can you practice listening this week?

2. What do you think you should be quick to listen to (1:19)?

_____

_____

_____

_____

_____

3. How do talkativeness and a quick temper hinder a person from listening (1:19)?

_____

_____

_____

_____

_____

4. Why doesn't human anger bring about the righteousness that God desires (James 1:20)? What is often wrong with our anger? (*Optional:* See Matthew 5:21-24,38-48; 6:14-15; 7:1-5; 1 John 3:15.)

_____

_____

_____

_____

_____

Humbly (1:21). "With meekness" in KJV. To be meek or humble is to accept what God commands and ordains, and to seek help from God rather than trusting in one's own abilities. It is not a passive tolerance of injustice (especially toward others), but a reliance on God for vindication and a refusal to retaliate when insulted.

The meek person is convinced that God's ways are good, so he neither disputes nor resists what God sends.

The humble person does not have a low opinion of himself; he is "not occupied with self at all."[1] Because he trusts God's goodness and His control over situations, the meek person does not have to worry about self-interest, "looking out for Number One," or enhancing his status.

Jesus' meekness (Matthew 11:29) did not conflict with His courage, concern for justice, and confidence that through God He was competent to do His job.

Perfect law that gives freedom (1:25). The moral teaching of Christianity is based on the Old Testament moral law of the Ten Commandments. The Old Testament Law was "perfect, reviving the soul" (Psalm 19:7); it was a complete, flawless expression of how people should treat God and each other. It was also "perfectly suited to our nature and situation."[2] Following the Law nurtured a person's soul by keeping him near God. However, men kept the Law imperfectly, but Christ has fulfilled the Law and enables us to fulfill it (Romans 8:4). Thus, He has made it truly perfect.

The "law of liberty" (KJV) is the law that applies to us who are freed from sin and selfishness. (See also Psalm 119:45 and John 8:31-36.) People often think that God's laws restrict us, but in fact, keeping them through Christ's power frees us more and more from sin to be what we were created to be (Romans 6:14-23).

For Further Study:
a. What kinds of things make God angry? (For example, see Exodus 4:1-17, 32:7-14; Deuteronomy 1:26-36; Zechariah 1:2-4; Mark 3:1-6.)
b. How is God's anger righteous?
c. When is it right for us to be angry (Ephesians 4:26)?

Optional Application: If you are angry with someone, apply Matthew 5:38-48 and 6:14-15. Ask God to enable you.

For Further Study: Study *humility* or *meekness* in cross-references, using a concordance. For example, what do you learn from Matthew 5:5; Galatians 5:23; Ephesians 4:2; 2 Timothy 2:25; Titus 3:2; 1 Peter 2:18; 3:4,15?

5. Summarize what James says about the Word in 1:18,21-22.

_____

_____

_____

_____

_____

47

For Thought and Discussion: a. In what sense is God's Word "planted in" us (1:21)? How does this implanting take place?

b. God and Christ are both called our Saviors in Scripture. In what sense does God's Word save our souls? How does this happen?

For Thought and Discussion: What might cause a person to forget to do what the Word says? Why is it easy to listen to God's Word without doing what it says?

For Thought and Discussion: What does it mean to be blessed in what you do (1:25)? In your judgment, does it mean guaranteed financial prosperity? Take the rest of Scripture into account.

6. How is a man who hears without doing like a man who looks in a mirror and later forgets (1:23-24)?

_____

_____

_____

_____

_____

7. How can you avoid forgetting what God's Word tells you about yourself and what you should do (1:25)?

_____

_____

_____

_____

_____

8. What does God promise to those who remember and do what they have heard (1:25)?

_____

_____

_____

_____

Religion (1:26-27). In common Jewish and Greek usage, pure and undefiled religion meant ceremonially clean and technically correct temple service and cultic acts. Both Jews and Greeks practiced ritual washing and used consecrated clothes and utensils to assure cleanness. Many pagan cults required abstinence from sexual contact before sacrifice, and the Jewish Law restricted contact with dead bodies, blood, and other substances (Leviticus 11:1-15:33).

48

James's definition of pure religion is a rejection (probably intentional) of this idea of external purity.

9. List some of the differences between worthless religion and pure, faultless religion (1:26-27).

worthless religion	pure religion

10. What one aspect of God's Word in 1:19-27 would you like to concentrate on this week?

_____

_____

_____

_____

_____

11. How do you see this truth already at work in your life?

_____

_____

_____

_____

_____

For Thought and Discussion: What does it mean to "keep oneself from being polluted by the world" (1:27)?

Optional Application: What pollutions of the world are the biggest dangers for you? What practical steps can you take?

Optional Application: Do you know any fatherless children or husband-less women? How can you help look out for them (or other needy people) in their distress (1:27)?

For Further Study:
Add 1:19-27 to your
outline of James.

12. How do you fall short or need to grow in this
    area? (Be as specific as possible.)

    _____

    _____

    _____

    _____

    _____

    _____

13. What can you do this week to be a doer of this
    truth, acting on it and beginning to make it a
    habit?

    _____

    _____

    _____

    _____

    _____

    _____

14. How can you make sure you remember to do
    this?

    _____

    _____

    _____

    _____

15. If you have any questions about 1:9-27 or this
    lesson, write them here.

    _____

    _____

    _____

    _____

For the group

Warm-up. Ask everyone to name one inner or outer thing that keeps him or her from always doing what God's Word says. Don't let people just say "sin"— ask them to explain what they mean in their own words.

Read aloud and summarize.

Questions. You may want to choose just a few of James's admonitions to discuss in depth. Have the group explain the meanings in members' own words. Have people tell how they do this or need to do this. Urge each person to commit to taking at least one practical step of doing what the Word says this week. Plan to share next week how things went. Stress that the purpose of sharing this is to encourage and help each other, not to impress or embarrass each other.

Worship. Thank God for the perfect law that gives freedom. Ask God for grace for each of you to do what His Word says. Pray about the specific commitments to application you have made today.

1. "Meek," W. E. Vine, *An Expository Dictionary of New Testament Words,* (Nashville, Tennessee: Royal Publishers, 1952), page 728. See also Wolfgang Bauder, "Humility, Meekness," *The New International Dictionary of New Testament Theology,* edited by Colin Brown, Volume 2 (Grand Rapids, Michigan: Zondervan Corporation, 1976), pages 256-259.
2. J. A. Motyer, *The Tests of Faith* (London: Inter-Varsity Press, 1970), page 36.

JAMES 2:1-13

No Favorites

It's easy to tell flabby from genuine Christian life, says James. The believer who is heading toward spiritual maturity is persevering while his faith is tested, is asking God for wisdom to deal with trials, and above all is listening to God's wise words and doing what He says. And what is this maturing Christian doing? Of the many tests of genuineness James could have named, he gives us three in 1:26-27. But exactly what do these tests of true religion—true faith—mean? James explains each one further in chapters 2 through 4. Consistently, he roots what we must *do* in who God *is* and who we *are*. Look for these themes as you read 2:1-13.

1. What three tests of true religion—genuine faith—does James list in 1:26-27?

   _____

   _____

   _____

2. What is James's main point in 2:1-13?

   _____

   _____

   _____

   _____

For Thought and Discussion: a. What does it mean to show favoritism or partiality?

b. Can you think of any times when you or your church have shown favoritism? If so, ask God to forgive you for these and commit yourself to avoid favoritism in the future. Ask God to enable you to do this. Watch for any temptations to show favoritism this week.

Optional Application: The next time you are at work or in church, make a point of greeting those whom you usually don't.

3. Which of the three tests does James seem to be elaborating on in this passage?

_____

_____

4. Do poor or shabby people come to your church? If so, how are they treated? If not, why do you think they don't come?

_____

_____

_____

_____

5. Why shouldn't we show favoritism to the rich?

2:1 _____

_____

_____

_____

2:4 (compare Matthew 7:1-2) _____

_____

_____

_____

2:5 (compare Luke 6:20) _____

_____

_____

_____

2:6-7 _____

_____

_____

_____

54

2:8-11 _____

_____

_____

Discriminated among yourselves (2:4). The Greek word rendered "discriminated" here is the same as the one translated "doubt" in 1:6. This word has the sense of "wavering" (1:6, KJV) or being "divided" (2:4, Revised Version). The Bible does not speak against discernment or discrimination based on valid standards; for instance, we should distinguish true teachers from false on the basis of their lives and characters (Matthew 7:15-23). Discrimination or judgment is bad when it springs from our divided, wavering values. To discriminate according to wealth is to mix worldly values with heavenly ones, to try to serve both God and Mammon (Matthew 6:24). This is the essence of the double-minded, unstable character James wants to root out of his readers (1:8).[1]

Exploiting you . . . dragging you into court (2:6). The book of Acts and other early documents confirm that it was more likely to be wealthy people who both felt threatened enough by Christianity and had the time and influence to cause trouble for believers. With a few exceptions, the rich and powerful have caused most of the persecutions throughout Christian history.

---

6. a. What might lead a person or group to treat rich people better than poor ones?

_____

_____

_____

_____

_____

Optional Application: Have you ever been the poor person treated condescendingly in a church? How did that make you feel about God? What did you do?

For Thought and Discussion: Why is it inconsistent for a believer "in our glorious Lord Jesus Christ" to show favoritism? Consider how Christ acted.

For Thought and Discussion: Who are currently leading the attacks on Christianity? Are they well-off, well-educated people or poor people? How should this affect our attitudes and actions (2:1-7)? Should we discriminate against the rich?

For Further Study:
Study how Jesus treated the poor and the working class (Luke 5:27-31, 14:12-14, 15:1-7). How is this a model for you? How can you follow it?

For Further Study:
What is God's attitude toward races and classes (Acts 10:34-35, Romans 2:9-11, Ephesians 6:9)?

For Thought and Discussion: Does James 2:12-13 contradict the idea that believers will be judged by mercy and grace rather than by strict justice and the Law? (See Matthew 5:7, Luke 6:38, Romans 2:6-11, 2 Corinthians 5:10, Galatians 6:7-10.)

b. What is wrong with the motives you just listed?

_____

_____

_____

_____

_____

_____

7. What is "the royal law" (2:8)?

_____

_____

_____

Royal law (2:8). This law is royal because it is one of the primary laws of the Kingdom of God, because it was proclaimed and confirmed by the King Himself, and because it rules and encompassed all the other laws of the Kingdom (Matthew 22:34-40, Romans 13:8-10).

8. Why does breaking one of God's laws make us guilty of breaking the whole (James 2:10-11)? (Consider what we are saying about God when we break a law. *Optional:* See Matthew 5:17-20,48; 22:34-40; Romans 13:8-10.)

_____

_____

_____

_____

_____

_____

56

Judged by the law that gives freedom (2:12).
Christ's law offers us the power to obey it, so it frees us from guaranteed condemnation (Romans 8:1-13). When we stand before Christ's judgment seat, we cannot plead that we are unable to obey the royal law. Also, by committing ourselves to Christ we freely pledged to obey Him, so we cannot claim that His law is a harsh burden imposed on us.[2] Our freedom as God's children and friends means more responsibility than when we were slaves to sin.

Law and grace are not contradictory. God gave Israel the Ten Commandments after He graciously liberated the people from slavery in Egypt. The laws were a gift to show how the redeemed should live. Likewise, after God frees us by grace from slavery to sin and death, He gives us commandments by which we may live abundant lives (Romans 6:15-23, 8:2). If we ignore those laws, we inevitably fall back into slavery to sin. (See also the definition for 1:25 on page 47.)

For Thought and Discussion: In the context of 2:1-13, what kind of mercy is James saying we should practice?

For Thought and Discussion: How do favoritism and discrimination show that we love ourselves more than others?

Optional Application: Toward whom do you need to show mercy this week, rather than prejudice, indifference, or resentment? How can you treat that person with mercy?

9. Specifically how should you "speak and act as those who are going to be judged by the law that gives freedom" (2:12) in your current circumstances?

_____

_____

_____

_____

10. What will happen to those of us who have not shown mercy to the needy, and why (James 2:13)? (*Optional:* See Matthew 5:7 and Luke 6:38.)

_____

_____

_____

**Optional
Application:** How
can you help see that
the poor are wel-
comed into your
church or fellowship?

_____

_____

_____

11. In this context, why is it personally important
to you that "mercy triumphs over judgment"
(2:13)?

_____

_____

_____

_____

_____

12. What one truth from 2:1-13 impresses you as
something you need to apply?

_____

_____

_____

_____

_____

13. How do you fall short or need to grow in this
area?

_____

_____

_____

_____

_____

14. What can you do this week to begin taking this
truth to heart and putting it into practice?

_____

_____

_____

_____

_____

For Further Study:
Add 2:1-13 to your
outline of James.

15. List any questions you have about 2:1-13.

_____

_____

_____

_____

For the group

Warm-up. Take time to share how last week's efforts to apply went. Does anyone have questions or need help, advice, or prayer? What obstacles to meditating on Scripture, remembering to do what you planned, etc. did you encounter? What successes did you experience? Encourage everyone not to expect overnight change, but to keep on persevering.

Question 1 is a good warm-up, but don't take a lot of time to criticize or praise your churches. Save your time for constructive planning when you discuss applications.

Questions. Spend a good portion of your time examining the motives that tempt people to favoritism and the circumstances that do or don't make poorer people feel welcome in a fellowship or church. Churches today are sometimes filled with people of one economic group because they all live in one neighborhood. But there can be other reasons. People may feel more comfortable with others of similar lifestyles. How godly is this? Some people feel it is not their responsibility to welcome visitors. Is this godly? Make some plans for ways to welcome strangers, especially the poor. Or, come up with other concrete ways of keeping the royal law and not showing favoritism.

Worship. Praise your Brother and Master, your "glorious Lord Jesus Christ." Praise Him for the way He treats you and all people, rich and poor. Thank

59

Him for treating you with mercy. Ask Him to help you do the same.

1. Motyer, pages 25, 43-44; Tasker, pages 42, 58.
2. Tasker, page 62; Motyer, pages 51-52.

JAMES 2:14-26

Genuine Faith

Is all this doing the Word and keeping the royal law really necessary? After all, since we are justified by faith in Christ (Romans 3:21-4:25, Ephesians 2:8-9), why bother with these works? Anyone who thinks this, James might have said, does not understand what our Lord Jesus and our brother Paul mean by faith.

Read 2:14-26 and review what James has already said about faith in 1:2-4.

1. On your first reading, what seems to be James's main point in 2:14-26?

_____

_____

_____

_____

_____

2. In the following chart, write down what Paul, John, Jesus, and James each says about faith and deeds.

   a. Paul says that we are saved by putting faith in Christ as our Lord and Savior. According to Paul, what kind of faith "counts" as genuine, saving faith (Galatians 5:6)?

For Further Study:
Does Paul agree or
disagree with James
in Romans 13:8-10,
Galatians 5:22-25,
and Philippians
2:12-13? Explain.

**Optional
Application:** Do you
ever say pious words
of encouragement but
neglect to do anything
practical to help
people in need? Do
you talk more about
the poor than you do
for them? If so, what
can you do to take
2:15-16 to heart?

b. According to the Apostle John, what is a crucial piece of evidence that we "belong to the
truth" and are children of God (1 John
3:10,17-19)?

c. What does Jesus say about faith and deeds in
Matthew 7:15-23, 25:31-46?

d. How does James show agreement with Paul
and John (James 1:27, 2:14-17)?

Paul	John
Jesus	James

Can such faith save him? (2:14). The impression
that James and Paul are in conflict comes partly
from the KJV translation of this phrase: "can
faith save him?" The point is "Can this kind of
passive, professed, but undemonstrated faith
save him?"

You have faith; I have deeds (2:18). Someone might object to James that "you" (some people) have the gift of faith, while "I" (other people) have the gift of good works. This would be a distortion of Paul's teaching about different parts of the body in Romans 12:4-8 and 1 Corinthians 12:4-11.[1] James insists (and Paul would agree) that every real Christian has faith *and* works.

There is one God (2:19). Or, "God is one" (RSV). This was the core of Jewish faith, recited daily in the form of the *Shema*, Deuteronomy 6:4-5. Jesus quoted part of this creed as the greatest commandment (Matthew 22:37). The belief in one God was the primary thing that set Jews and Christians apart from pagans.

Optional Application: How can you avoid the wrong believing of the demons?

For Further Study:
a. Read Genesis 22:1-18 for the story James discusses in James 2:21-24.
b. See how Paul uses Abraham as an example of faith in Romans 4:1-25.
c. See how Abraham is an example of true faith in Hebrews 11:8-19.

3. James 2:16 is an example of dead or worthless faith that doesn't save. James gives another example in 2:19.

   a. What do the demons believe about God (2:19)?

   _____

   _____

   _____

   b. What is wrong with the demon's faith? How is it like human faith that produces no good deeds?

   _____

   _____

   _____

   _____

   _____

   _____

Abraham (2:21). God promised Abraham a son from whom he would receive countless descendants (Genesis 12:1-3, 15:1-5). Even though Abraham

Optional Application: Abraham showed faith by holding nothing back from God, not even his most valued treasure. Are you holding anything back from God? Is there anything you wouldn't sacrifice for Him? Pray about this.

Optional Application: Rahab showed faith by caring for Israelites in danger. How could you follow this example?

was about eighty years old, he believed God, and God counted him righteous because of his faith (Genesis 15:6). Twenty years later, the promised son was finally born. But when Isaac was a teenager, God commanded Abraham to sacrifice his son (Genesis 22:1-18). Abraham had to risk all his dreams on the conviction that God would keep His promises—to the extent of resurrecting Isaac, if necessary.

Righteous . . . justified (2:21,24-25). For Paul, to be justified is to be made righteous in God's sight. It is salvation, the beginning of Christian life from God's point of view. In James's terms, to be justified is to be shown to have the kind of real faith that saves. A justified person has proven to people that he is righteous. Faith makes us righteous (justified in Paul's terms); works motivated by faith show that we are righteous (justified in James's usage).[2]

Rahab (2:25). This Canaanite prostitute decided that the God of Israel was more worthy of her allegiance than the idols of Canaan. She showed her new loyalty by risking her life to protect two Israelites from the king of Jericho (Joshua 2:1-24).

4. James offers Abraham and Rahab as two examples of genuine faith. What did Abraham's willingness to sacrifice Isaac prove (Genesis 22:12, James 2:22-23)?

_____

_____

_____

_____

5. How does Abraham reflect what James says about faith in 1:2-4?

_____

_____

_____

_____

_____

6. In summary, why is faith that is not demon-
strated with deeds dead?

_____

_____

_____

_____

_____

7. In your own words, summarize the relationship
between faith and works.

_____

_____

_____

_____

_____

_____

8. What truth from 2:14-26 most stands out to you
as something that should affect your life?

_____

_____

_____

_____

_____

9. How do you fall short in this area, or how do
you want it to affect your life?

_____

_____

For Thought and Discussion:
a. Are all good deeds evidence of faith in Jesus (Matthew 7:22-23)? Why or why not?
   b. Do good deeds not motivated by faith in Jesus have any value in God's eyes? Why or why not?
   c. Is there any way to demonstrate true faith other than by deeds of obedience to God? Why or why not?

For Thought and Discussion: If deeds demonstrate genuine faith, can we judge by their works whether other people are saved? Why or why not? (Consider what Jesus says in Matthew 7:1-5,15-21.)

For Thought and Discussion: a. Jesus said "by their fruit you will recognize" true and false believers (Matthew 7:20). In your judgment, how quickly should a new believer begin to show the fruit of a changed life? Explain your reasoning.

b. How is it possible to show the fruit of genuine faith (John 15:1-5)?

10. What can you do to begin putting this truth into practice?

_____

_____

_____

_____

_____

11. List any questions you have about 2:14-26.

_____

_____

_____

_____

For the group

Warm-up. Ask each person to think of one way in which people can tell that he or she has faith in Jesus.

Read aloud and summarize.

Questions. Since some people have been confused into thinking that James denies Paul's doctrine of justification by faith apart from works, this lesson focuses on how James, Paul, John, and Jesus are in agreement. Lead the group to the point where you can all state clearly what the relationship between faith and works is.

Then, apply James's words to yourselves. Remember that his emphasis is active and practical, not passive and theoretical. Think of some specific ways in which each of you, or all of you as a group, can demonstrate your faith with deeds. Consider especially the kinds of deeds James stresses in chapter 2: loving your neighbor as yourself (2:8), caring for the needy (2:16), giving God whatever He asks without resentment (2:21), risking your comfort and safety for others in need (2:25). Or, look for ways of avoiding the false faith James condemns: pious words without action (2:16), or doctrinal accuracy combined with malice toward God and His people (2:19).

For Further Study: Add 2:14-26 to your outline.

Summarize. How is 2:14-26 related to what James has already said? Consider 1:2-4,22,27; 2:1-4,8,12. Are you getting a grip on James's overall message?

Worship. Praise God for what you believe about Him—that He is the only God, that He has saved you by grace despite your sin, etc. Thank Him that you can demonstrate your real heart beliefs by what you do. Thank Him for the examples of Abraham and Rahab. Ask Him to show you how you can better live out your faith.

1. Tasker, pages 64-66; Motyer, page 55.
2. Tasker, pages 67-68; Warren Wiersbe, *Be Mature* (Wheaton, Illinois: Victor Books, 1978), page 83.

JAMES 3:1-12

Controlling the Tongue

One sure sign of true or worthless faith is what comes out of a person's mouth. Jesus says, "out of the overflow of the heart the mouth speaks," so "by your words you will be acquitted, and by your words you will be condemned" (Matthew 12:34,37). For Jesus, this is one of the chief fruits by which we can discern true believers from false ones (Matthew 12:33-37).

All of us will be judged by our words, but none of us more than teachers. Being a rabbi in Jewish culture meant power, privilege, and respect, but Jesus told His disciples not to be called "Rabbi," "Father," or "Teacher" (Matthew 23:8-12). James has similar counsel. In chapter 3 he comes to his second test of pure religion (1:26), of living faith (2:26), of maturity (3:2)—the use of the tongue. Read 3:1-12.

1. Why should we hesitate before we presume to be teachers (James 3:1)? (*Optional:* Consider Matthew 12:33-37, Romans 2:17-24.)

   _____

   _____

   _____

   _____

   _____

For Further Study:
What does Matthew
23:1-12 have to say
to Christian teachers?

**For Thought and
Discussion:** The
tongue is "set on fire
by hell" (James 3:6),
and Satan is "the
father of lies" (John
8:44). Does this
mean that Satan, not
we, is responsible for
our evil words? Why
or why not? (Consider
the rest of John 8:44.)

Perfect (3:2). This is the same Greek word as
"mature" in 1:4 and "complete" in 2:22 (KJV has
"perfect" in all three verses). The word means
"that which has reached its maturity or fulfilled
the end contemplated."[1] God's goal for us is
holiness and righteousness like His (Matthew
5:48, Ephesians 4:22-24). We may not reach
that goal in this life, but we should be growing
toward it.

2. James uses some vivid imagery to explain why
   controlling our tongues is the key to maturity.
   How is a tongue like a horse's bit or a ship's
   rudder (3:2-5)?

   _____

   _____

   _____

   _____

   _____

   _____

A world of evil among the parts of the body (3:6).
Or, "*the* world of evil." The tongue represents
and expresses the fallen world order in our
bodies perhaps more than any other organ.[2]

The whole course of his life (3:6). This is the prob-
able meaning of "the course of nature" (KJV).

3. Put into your own words what James says about
   the tongue in 3:6.

   _____

   _____

   _____

   _____

_____

_____

_____

_____

_____

For Thought and Discussion: To what kinds of speech does 3:9 apply, besides actual swearing?

For Thought and Discussion: a. What would happen to the fresh water if fresh and salt water flowed from the same spring (3:11)?

b. How is this like what happens to our praises if curses also come from our mouths (3:10)?

Restless (3:8). Like a wild beast ready to break out of its cage at any time.[3]

4. Animals can be tamed because God gave man dominion over them at Creation (Genesis 1:26-28, James 3:7). Why can't man tame his own tongue (Genesis 2:16-17, 6:5; James 3:8)?

_____

_____

_____

_____

_____

5. Why is it especially horrible to curse or verbally abuse a human being (James 3:9)?

_____

_____

_____

_____

_____

6. How does James depict the idea of doubleness (1:8) with respect to the tongue (3:10-12)?

_____

_____

_____

For Further Study:
For more on question
9, see Matthew
12:33-34; Luke
11:5-13, 18:1-8;
Romans 8:1-14;
Ephesians 3:14-21.

_____

_____

7. Back in 3:2, James said that the person who can control his tongue is perfect, mature. From 3:1-12, why is this so?

_____

_____

_____

_____

8. James says it isn't possible for a human to attain perfection by completely taming his tongue (3:8). How, then, can we control our tongues and become mature (Matthew 19:25-26, James 1:5-8)?

_____

_____

_____

_____

9. Bearing your answer to question 8 in mind, what can a person do to become more godly in what he or she says? (*Optional:* See John 15:5-8, Romans 6:11-14, James 4:6-10.)

_____

_____

_____

_____

_____

_____

10. What one insight from 3:1-12 would you like to take to heart?

_____

_____

_____

_____

_____

11. How do you need to grow in this area?

_____

_____

_____

_____

12. With your answers to question 9 in mind, write some plans for acting on this insight.

_____

_____

_____

_____

_____

_____

13. List any questions you have about 3:1-12.

_____

_____

_____

_____

For Further Study:
a. Study and meditate on ways people misuse their tongues. See, for instance, Proverbs 6:16-17; 10:19; 12:22; 17:9,27; 18:13; 19:9; 20:19; 26:20,28; 27:2; 28:23; 29:5,20.
   b. Study some positive uses of the tongue, such as in Romans 10:14-15 and Colossians 3:15-17.

For the group

Warm-up. Ask everyone to think of the last really edifying, loving thing he or she said. Then ask every-

For Further Study: Add 3:1-12 to your outline.

one to think of the last hurtful thing he or she said.

Read aloud and summarize.

Questions. Most people will quickly agree that their tongues are out of control and often harmful. So, you should be able to cover questions 1-7 relatively quickly. Spend a large part of your time discussing what you can and should do to begin ruling your tongues. Commit yourselves to praying for each other this week.

Worship. Pray seriously for the grace to turn your tongues over to God's control. Thank Him for providing the power to control what you cannot. Confess and ask forgiveness for ways in which you have verbally abused people who have been made in God's likeness.

1. Marvin R. Vincent, *Word Studies in the New Testament*, volume 1 (Grand Rapids, Michigan: William B. Eerdmans Publishing Company, 1946), page 724.
2. Tasker, pages 75-76.
3. Motyer, page 67.

JAMES 3:13-18

Wisdom

"Not many of you should presume to be teachers,"
says James, because we all make mistakes and
teachers' mistakes will be judged most strictly
(3:1-2). Still, many of us do claim to have the wisdom and knowledge necessary to instruct our
neighbors. Even those of us who wouldn't dream of
preaching in public are often full of advice for our
friends. James has some words for all of us professional and amateur teachers. Read 3:13-18.

Wise and understanding (3:13). Recall the meaning
of "wisdom" from 1:5 (page 27). Wisdom is
essentially practical, even when it is about
spiritual things. The Greek word rendered
"understanding" in NIV means to be equipped
with "expert or professional knowledge."[1]
Together, to be wise and understanding means
to know all the technical facts, all the spiritual
implications, and all the practical applications
that a teacher needs.

Humility (3:13). On humility see page 46.

1. How can we recognize (in ourselves and in others) the wisdom and understanding necessary
for a teacher (3:13)?

_____

_____

_____

_____

2. Jesus encouraged people to come learn from Him because He was "gentle and humble in heart" (Matthew 11:29). Paul asserted his authority as an apostle and teacher after invoking "the meekness and gentleness of Christ" (2 Corinthians 10:1). Why do you think humility or meekness is such an essential sign of wisdom?

_____

_____

_____

_____

_____

_____

3. Explain in your own words what the following are:

bitter envy (3:14) _____

_____

_____

_____

selfish ambition (3:14) _____

_____

_____

_____

4. How do bitter envy and selfish ambition affect a person's ministry?

_____

_____

_____

_____

_____

Wisdom (3:15-17). Wisdom is chiefly a matter of means, not ends. Thus, there is a kind of wisdom that leads a person to live in a way that heads toward eternal life, and a kind that leads him toward eternal death. Clever, successful people may indeed be wise in how to attain their goals, but James casts doubt on their goals.

5. Contrast the effects of the wisdom that is "earthly, unspiritual, of the devil" (3:15-16) with those of the wisdom that comes from God (3:17-18).

earthly, unspiritual, of the devil	heavenly, spiritual, of God

Disorder (3:16). This word suggests primarily mental confusion,[2] but mental disarray inevitably brings outward disorder and **every evil practice**. It is the same word rendered "unstable" in 1:8.

77

For Thought and Discussion: Do you think a peacemaker avoids conflict at all costs? Does he end debate by imposing his solution on others? Does he always give in when opposed? Explain your reasoning.

That is, earthly wisdom leads to that same inconsistent, wavering doubleness that James has been preaching against.[3]

6. Why do you think envy and selfish ambition lead to disorder and evil practices? (*Optional:* See Romans 1:18-32, Ephesians 4:17-19.)

_____

_____

_____

_____

_____

_____

Considerate (3:17). "Gentle" in KJV and RSV. This is to be thoughtful, forbearing, not concerned with one's own rights. A gentle or considerate person "will rather take sides against himself, look from the other's point of view, remember his own duties and the other's rights." He "will yield like air in matters of personal feeling or interest," but "will stand like rock in respect of moral principle."[4]

Submissive (3:17). "Easy to be intreated" in KJV; "open to reason" in RSV. Such a person does not necessarily give in to every demand made of him, but he is open to discussion, negotiation, and requests. He is not stubborn, short-tempered, or autocratic.

7. In contrast to the maker of disorder (3:16) is the maker of peace (3:17-18). In light of 3:13-18, what do you think it means to be a peacemaker?

_____

_____

_____

_____

_____

_____

For Further Study:
Add 3:13-18 to your outline.

8. Sowing in peace produces a harvest of righteousness (3:18). Why do you suppose peacemaking and righteousness are connected like this?

_____

_____

_____

_____

_____

_____

9. All the good traits of 3:17-18 spring from acquiring heavenly wisdom and ridding ourselves of devilish wisdom. How can you cultivate heavenly wisdom and its fruits this week?

a. Are there any traits or habits you need to repent of? If so, write them down and confess them to God.

_____

_____

_____

_____

_____

b. What else can you do to grow in heavenly wisdom? Be as specific about your plans as possible. (*Optional:* See your answers to questions 8 and 9 of lesson seven [page 72]. You might also consider Job 28:28, Psalm 119:9-16, Proverbs 8:12, Romans 8:5-8, James 1:5-8.)

_____

_____

_____

_____

_____

_____

10. List any questions you have about 3:13-18.

_____

_____

_____

_____

_____

For the group

Warm-up. Ask everyone, "Are you a person who tends to give advice and counsel to others, or do you avoid doing this?" If you know and trust each other, let the other group members give feedback to each person about how much advice they have seen him or her give.

Read aloud and summarize.

Questions. Much of this lesson is a matter of examining what various words and phrases mean. Get the group to give concise definitions and examples if possible. You might want to bring a dictionary for definitions. For examples, avoid a judgmental attitude toward people you think reflect earthly wisdom. Focus on people you think show heavenly wisdom.

    Then help each other to be honest about your own wisdom. How well do you each display it? How can you acquire more of the right kind of wisdom? What attitudes and priorities have been getting in the way, and what can you do about these?

Worship. Thank God for showing and offering you His kind of wisdom. Spend some time praying that God will give each of you heavenly wisdom and its fruits.

1. Tasker, page 79.
2. Tasker, page 81.
3. Motyer, page 75.
4. C. G. Moule, *The Epistle to the Philippians*, (Grand Rapids, Michigan: Baker Book House, 1981), page 80.

JAMES 4:1-10

Whose Friend?

Earthly wisdom causes disorder, but heavenly wisdom leads to peace (3:15-18). So why don't we have peace in our homes, jobs, and churches? Perhaps we are operating with the wrong kind of wisdom. For some tough heavenly insights on this problem, read 4:1-10.

For Further Study:
See other conditions for answered prayer in Psalm 34:15, 145:18; Luke 18:14; John 15:7; 1 John 5:14.

1. What causes us to fight and quarrel (4:1-2)?

_____

_____

_____

_____

2. When we ask God for things, why do we often not get what we want (4:3)?

_____

_____

_____

_____

Desires (4:1). Literally, "pleasures" as in 4:3. The Greek word *hedonon* gives us the word *hedonism*. James is not saying that the pleasures of

83

Optional Application: What desires battle within you, against you? Is pleasure or God the dominant concern of your life? Examine your actions, and ask God to show you yourself as you really are.

For Thought and Discussion: How does it affect you to know that God considers your pursuit of selfish goals to be adultery?

this life war against each other ("as though man's main problem consisted in making a choice between higher and lower kinds of pleasure"[1]). Rather, they battle within us, against our will to put aside selfishness and serve others.

---

3. Describe a time in your life when you have done and experienced something James describes in 4:1-3.

_____

_____

_____

_____

_____

Adulterous people (4:4). Literally, "adulteresses." (Not, as in KJV, "adulterers and adulteresses.") In the Old Testament, God often describes Himself as the Husband of His people (Isaiah 54:6-8, Jeremiah 31:32, Ezekiel 16:1-63, Hosea 2:2), and the New Testament calls the Church Bride of Christ (Ephesians 5:25-32; Revelation 19:7, 21:2). Thus, to pursue the world's pleasures is to commit adultery against our Husband.

World (4:4). The Greek word *kosmos* has to do with order. It can mean the physical universe or earth, but more often it refers to the human world system or the evil world system.[2] God "so loved the world" (John 3:16) that He sent Jesus to be "the Savior of the world" (1 John 4:14) in the sense of saving people who are in the human world system. In James 1:27, 3:6, and 4:4, James means the evil world system—the world order of humans in rebellion against God, led by "the prince of this world" (John 12:31, 16:11). Keeping oneself from being polluted by the world is one of James's tests of pure religion (James 1:27). He elaborates on this test in chapter 4.

84

4. From your experience and knowledge of the Scriptures, what are some of the symptoms of friendship with the world?

_____

_____

_____

_____

_____

_____

5. Why is friendship with the world equivalent to hatred toward God (James 4:4)? (*Optional:* See Luke 16:13; Romans 8:5-8; 1 John 2:15-17, 3:8.)

_____

_____

_____

_____

_____

_____

Optional Application: Do you recognize any of the symptoms of friendship with the world in your own life? If so, what can you do about it?

For Further Study: For more on the humility that wins grace, see 1 Peter 5:5-7.

The spirit . . . envies intensely (4:5). The variations among modern versions reflects the difficulty of translating this verse. There are at least three possibilities:

1. "The spirit he caused to live in us envies intensely" (NIV): God caused our human spirit to live in us when He breathed on man in creation (Genesis 2:7). Because of the Fall, our human spirit is corrupted and "envies intensely." But God's grace (James 4:6) can overcome man's envy.[3]

2. "God jealously longs for the spirit that he made to live in us" (NIV footnote): God jealously longs for our spirits to respond to Him with faithfulness and love. God's grace is able to accomplish this.

3. "The Spirit he caused to live in us longs

Optional Application: How can you actively submit to God today or tomorrow?

Optional Application: In what areas do you need to resist the devil today?

For Further Study: On resisting the devil, see Matthew 4:1-11, Ephesians 6:10-18, 1 Peter 5:6-11, 1 John 5:18.

jealously" (NIV footnote): The Holy Spirit in us Christians longs for our faithfulness and love. Again, grace can achieve this.

6. Proverbs 3:34 says "God opposes the proud" (James 4:6). What is pride? (Recall the meaning of humility from page 46.)

_____

_____

_____

_____

_____

_____

_____

7. God provides plenty of grace for us to overcome our envy, craving for pleasure, and consequent quarreling (4:6). He offers abundant grace to respond to Him with full devotion.
   Why does He give us this grace only if we are humble, never if we are proud?

_____

_____

_____

_____

_____

_____

_____

Submit (4:7). Not a passive lying back and letting God do whatever He wants, but an active obedience to God's commands as a soldier submits to his general. Submission to God is as active as resistance of the devil.

8. What does each of the following commands have to do with pride and humility?

"Submit yourselves . . . to God" (4:7) _____

_____

_____

_____

_____

"Resist the devil" (4:7) _____

_____

_____

_____

_____

"Come near to God and he will come near to you" (4:8)

_____

_____

_____

_____

_____

"Wash your hands, you sinners, and purify your hearts, you double-minded" (4:8)

_____

_____

_____

_____

_____

"Grieve, mourn and wail. Change your laughter to mourning and your joy to gloom" (4:9)

_____

For Thought and Discussion: Have you ever wondered why you didn't feel God near to you? According to 4:8, is this a failure on God's part or on our part? What should we do when God seems far away?

Optional Application: a. Do your actions show that you are double-minded or single-minded in your devotion to God? Who does your behavior show is really first in your life? (Review what you have done for the past several days.)
    b. What can you do to grow more single-minded?

For Further Study:
Compare James 4:9
to Ecclesiastes
2:1-11; 7:2-4; Luke
6:20-21,24-25;
18:9-14. Does this
contradict James's
exhortation to be joy-
ful (1:2)? Why is grief
often appropriate for
Christians, and how
can we mourn our
sins without losing
joy?

9. How would you summarize James's main point in 4:1-10?

10. What one aspect of this passage would you like to apply to your own life?

11. How do you fall short or need to grow in this area?

12. What can you do to put this truth into practice this week?

For Further Study:
Add 4:1-10 to your
outline.

_____

_____

_____

_____

13. List any questions you have about 4:1-10.

_____

_____

_____

_____

For the group

Warm-up. Ask one or two people to answer this question: "Recall a recent quarrel you have had. What do you think caused it?"

Read aloud and summarize.

Questions. This lesson includes a lot of "why" questions. These are not for wild speculation, but for thinking that takes into account everything you know about Scripture and God. Listen to everyone's opinions, and gently discern any flaws or inconsistencies with the rest of Scripture. If you cannot answer "why," you can always simply accept a biblical statement. However, perceiving God's reasons for commands and statements often helps us understand Him better and obey Him more confidently. For example, seeing why He opposes the proud may enable you to uproot your own pride.

The "why" of a verse is often implicit in it. For instance, if we understand what the world is and what it stands for, we can see why friendship with it is enmity with God.

Don't neglect personal applications by miring yourself in the "whys." What can each of you do to put 4:1-10 into practice?

Worship. Praise God for opposing the proud but giving all necessary grace to the humble. Ask Him to help you each to submit to Him and resist the devil's temptations to pride and pleasure. Do some of the confessing, mourning, and humbling yourselves that James urges. Be specific and honest in your confessions.

1. Tasker, page 85.
2. Donald W. Burdick, *The Letters of John the Apostle* (Chicago: Moody Press, 1985), pages 176-177, 186-187.
3. *The NIV Study Bible*, page 1884.

JAMES 4:11-5:6

More on Pride

"God opposes the proud," quotes James from Proverbs 3:34 (James 4:6). Now he gives three examples of pride, along with specific reasons for humbling ourselves. Each reason is an example of the heavenly wisdom that keeps itself unpolluted by friendship with the world. And each is tied to the essential character of the Lord Himself.

Read 4:11-5:6.

Slander (4:11-12)

The first act of pride has to do with our nemesis, the tongue.

1. To slander or judge a brother is to criticize and judge God's Law (4:11). Why is this so? (See 2:8.)

_____

_____

_____

_____

_____

2. Why is this the height of pride (4:12)?

_____

For Thought and Discussion: a. Is it okay to speak against someone as long as we are sure it is the truth? Why or why not?

b. How is constructive criticism different from slander?

For Thought and Discussion: What do you think you should do if someone slanders another in your presence?

91

Optional Application:
a. Recall the last time you spoke against another person, especially a Christian. If you haven't already done so, confess your arrogance to God and ask for the grace to change.

b. Watch for and write down times this week when you do speak against or judge people. Try to stop and confess as soon as you can. If possible, apologize to the person you are talking to (slander defiles the hearer as well as the slandered one, and it encourages the hearer to imitate it). To keep the issue of slander in mind, meditate daily on 4:11-12.

For Further Study:
a. If we slander or accuse our brothers and sisters, whom are we like (Revelation 12:10)?

b. What does Christ do instead (1 John 2:1-2)?

c. What implications do these truths have for us?

_____

_____

_____

_____

Boasting (4:13-17)

So far, James has been talking about wrong views of the present. The next two examples of pride concern attitudes about the future. Money figures prominently, as it has before (1:9-11,27; 2:1-7,15-16; 4:1-3).

3. What attitude does James condemn in 4:13?

_____

_____

_____

_____

4. How is this proud and foolish (4:14)?

_____

_____

_____

_____

5. What is a person saying about God and self when he makes plans without consulting God?

_____

_____

_____

_____

6. What would be the humble attitude toward plans (4:15)?

_____

_____

_____

_____

_____

7. How is 4:17 relevant to 4:13-16?

_____

_____

_____

_____

_____

8. What other applications does 4:17 have to your life?

_____

_____

_____

_____

_____

_____

Hoarding (5:1-6)

9. What have some rich people done to get in big trouble (5:1-6)? List as many actions and attitudes as you can find.

_____

_____

_____

For Thought and Discussion: Is it always wrong to make plans for the future? If so, why? If not, what kinds of planning are wrong, and what kinds are all right? (*Optional:* See Matthew 6:25-33; Acts 18:21; 1 Corinthians 4:19, 16:3-9; James 4:15.)

For Thought and Discussion: Is saying "God willing" about every plan a guarantee that we have the right attitude? Why or why not?

Optional Application: What plans for the future are you living by? Assess them in light of 4:13-17. Have you taken into account the brevity of your life and God's right to direct your plans?

For Further Study:
On James 5:1-6, see
Luke 12:13-34,
16:19-31.

**For Thought and
Discussion:** Does
James seem to be
condemning all rich
people? If so, why? If
not, how can one be a
good rich person?

_____

_____

_____

_____

_____

10. Why does this earn them condemnation in "the
    day of slaughter" (5:5)? (See, for example,
    James 2:8,12-13 and Deuteronomy 10:17-21;
    15:10-11; 23:19-20; 24:10-15.)

_____

_____

_____

_____

_____

11. How is it a sign of pride and arrogance to do
    what James 5:1-6 describes?

_____

_____

_____

_____

Your response

12. What one warning, command, or truth from
    James 4:11-5:6 would you most like to take to
    heart?

_____

_____

_____

_____

_____

94

13. How do you fall short or need to grow in this area?

_____

_____

_____

_____

_____

14. What do you plan to do to act on this truth?

_____

_____

_____

_____

_____

15. List any questions you have about 4:11-5:6.

_____

_____

_____

_____

Optional Application: Are you hoarding wealth or living in self-indulgence rather than treating poorer people with justice and generosity? If so, what can you do about this?

For Further Study: Add 4:11-5:6 to your outline.

For the group

Warm-up. Ask everyone to recall the last time he or she criticized someone. It is not necessary to have people describe the situations aloud.

Read aloud and summarize.

Questions. This lesson relates each paragraph in 4:11-5:6 to pride in order to help you understand the pride and humility stressed in 4:6-10. Use this to organize your discussion and identify pride in yourselves. Confess your prideful attitudes, and look for ways to act with humility.

You could equally well relate each paragraph to earthly/heavenly wisdom or to friendship with

God/the world. For example, in 4:1-6, James describes wrong, worldly attitudes of earthly wisdom toward things, people, self, and God. In 4:7-5:6, he urges right, heavenly attitudes toward God, self, people, and things. If you like, make a chart showing "Earthly Attitudes" and "Heavenly Attitudes," noting which verses apply to each attitude.

Worship. Praise God for being the one Lawgiver and Judge, the one who decides what your futures will hold, the Lord Almighty who hears the cries of the oppressed. Humble yourselves before Him, confess you faults, and ask Him to give you each grace to practice what you have learned.

JAMES 5:7-20

Patience and Prayer

.

Most of James's readers are not the hardhearted rich he denounced in 5:1-6. They were more likely to be the workers mentioned in 5:4. To them are addressed the encouragements and warnings of 5:7-20.

For Further Study:
For more on patience, study Romans 12:19-20, James 1:19, 2 Peter 3:9-12.

Patience (5:7-12)

Patient (5:7). Patience is "not so much the brave endurance of afflictions . . . as the self-restraint which enables the sufferer to refrain from hasty retaliation. The opposites of 'patience' in this sense are wrath and revenge." Scripture uses this Greek word for God's patience—His slowness to punish us as we deserve, His generosity in giving time for us to repent, and His eagerness to make allowances. God's patience is the reason why ***the Lord's coming*** is delayed, for that will be the Day of Judgment. Since God is postponing that day out of patience, we too should be patient in awaiting justice. The alternatives—"vindictiveness and despair"— must both be rejected.[1]

1. The word "then" (NASB: "therefore") connects 5:7-12 to 5:1-6. Our patience should be based in part on what James said in that previous para-

For Thought and Discussion: Why shouldn't we lose patience with the Lord after almost two thousand years? (For example, see 2 Peter 3:3-15.)

For Thought and Discussion: What convictions enable farmers to wait patiently for rain? How are these relevant to your situation?

For Further Study: What do and don't we know about the time of Christ's return (Matthew 24:26-27,36-39)?

graph. Why would 5:1-6 lead to an exhortation to be patient?

_____

_____

_____

_____

_____

2. What are some of the circumstances that tempt you to lose patience?

_____

_____

_____

_____

_____

_____

Coming (5:7,8). Peter, Paul, John, and Jesus Himself all use the word *parousia* to refer to Jesus' second coming in glory. The word "was current among the Greeks to describe the official visits of a monarch to a city within his dominions. On such state occasions the royal 'presence' (for that is the literal meaning of the word) was such that none could fail to recognize the Sovereign for what in fact he was. By the use of this word . . . for the second coming of Christ, that second coming is contrasted with His first." The Man born in an animals' feed trough and executed as a criminal "came, so to speak, *incognito*." But when Christ returns in glory as Judge and Lord, there will be no doubting His identity (Revelation 1:7).[2]

Autumn and spring rains (5:7). "In Israel the autumn rain comes in October and November soon after the grain is sown, and the spring rain comes in March and April just prior to harvest."[3]

98

Near (5:8). John the Baptist's message was "Repent, for the kingdom of heaven is near" (Matthew 3:2). After Jesus was baptized and John was imprisoned, Jesus began to proclaim, "Repent, for the kingdom of heaven is near" (Matthew 4:17; compare Mark 1:15). The Kingdom was "at hand" (RSV), on the doorstep, because the King Himself was present. Jesus told His disciples to preach the same message (Matthew 10:7).

3. In what sense has the Lord's coming been "near" for the past two thousand years?

_____

_____

_____

_____

_____

4. Why should expecting the Lord's coming make you patient (5:7-9)?

_____

_____

_____

_____

_____

_____

For Thought and Discussion: Why does grumbling at others lead to judgment (5:9)? (*Optional:* See Matthew 7:1-6.)

Optional Application: Do you tend to grumble? If so, ask God to help you deal patiently with the people and circumstances you consider unjust. Try thanking God daily for everything you are grateful for (Philippians 4:4-9). Look for reasons to be grateful. Ask God to help you give Him all your anxieties (1 Peter 5:7).

For Thought and Discussion: What does it mean to "stand firm" (5:8), and how can we do this?

The prophets (5:10). Far from being a sign of God's disapproval, suffering was the experience of almost every prophet. Jeremiah, for instance, was beaten, held in the stocks, imprisoned in a pit, and nearly murdered.

Job's perseverance (5:11). KJV renders this as "patience," but it is a different word from the

For Further Study:
a. Read Job 1:1-2:11,
29:1-30:1, 42:1-17.
What is encouraging
to you about Job's
story?

b. Read Jeremiah
8:18-9:6, 20:1-18,
26:1-16, 36:1-43:13.
What encouragement
does Jeremiah's life
offer you?

For Further Study:
What did affliction do
to the writer of Psalm
119:67,71?

one in 5:7,10. Job was not patient in awaiting justice from God or his friends. However, he did show perseverance, endurance, "a determination to face a particular trial or a series of trials without flinching." Job was determined to endure his sufferings without losing faith in God. "He believed even when he could not understand."[4]

What the Lord finally brought about was not only a complete restoration of Job's health and possessions, but also "a fuller understanding of the mystery of the divine purpose, and a more direct experience of the majesty and sovereignty of Almighty God; and he became capable of a greater and deeper penitence."[5]

5. Why do we consider those who persevere under suffering to be blessed (5:11)? What are some of the blessings that follow such perseverance? (*Optional:* See James 1:12; Matthew 5:10-12; 10:24-25; Revelation 2:7,11,17,26-28; 3:5,12,21.)

_____

_____

_____

_____

_____

_____

6. Patience is not a quality we naturally possess. How can we acquire it (Galatians 5:22-23)?

_____

_____

_____

_____

_____

Swear (5:12). James is not talking primarily about "cussing" (although we might extend the passage to apply to cussing). In his day, people rarely signed written contracts for business and personal agreements. Instead, they swore oaths. The thing by which they swore supposedly bound them to keep their word. The Jewish teachers knew all kinds of legal loopholes for escaping from such oaths without breaking the Jewish law; Jesus condemned this practice (Matthew 23:16-22). But even common people were in the habit of swearing frivolously to validate their words, even invoking God's name to do so.

For Thought and Discussion: In your judgment, does James 5:12 forbid solemn oaths in court? Why or why not? (See Deuteronomy 4:26, 6:13; Jeremiah 12:16; Matthew 26:63-64; Romans 1:9, 9:1; 2 Corinthians 1:23; Galatians 1:20; 2 Timothy 4:1; Hebrews 6:13.)

7. Another sign of impatience is frivolous swearing (James 5:12). Why is it so offensive to God (Exodus 20:7, Matthew 5:33-37)?

_____

_____

_____

_____

_____

For Thought and Discussion: What does swearing, especially by using God's name, do to a person's witness before unbelievers? Why?

For Thought and Discussion: What heart attitudes do you think motivate people to swear oaths instead of just saying "yes" or "no"?

Prayer (5:13-18)

Elders . . . anoint him (5:14). In James's time, oil was used as a soothing medicine for wounds (Luke 10:34). Among Christians, it also symbolized the Holy Spirit (Acts 10:38, 1 John 2:20). Since the sick man is being anointed *in the name of the Lord*—invoking Jesus' power and authority—James probably has in mind both the medicinal and symbolic properties of the oil. A man of his time would not distinguish natural and supernatural means of healing, since all healing is from God. Indeed, it is not the oil that heals at all: *the prayer offered in faith will make the sick person well; the Lord will raise*

For Further Study:
a. As guidance for prayer in affliction, study and meditate on some of the following: Luke 18:1, 22:39-44; 2 Corinthians 12:7-10; 1 Peter 5:10.
   b. What should we remember when we are afflicted (Romans 8:18, 2 Corinthians 4:17-18)?
   c. What results if we allow afflictions to cause bitterness instead of prayer (Hebrews 12:15)?

him up (5:15). Physical actions like anointing and touching with hands were common accompaniments to prayer among Jews, and they were carefully distinguished from magic rituals.

This passage has been applied in various ways over the centuries. Between the third and ninth centuries AD, the Roman Catholic Church gradually shifted from letting lay people anoint the sick whenever they desired to allowing only priests to anoint only dying people. The practice became a last rite to forgive the dying, rather than a rite for healing the sick. Since 1974, the Roman Catholic Rite of Anointing stresses that lay people should be involved and may anoint the sick, and that the rite is for healing.[6]

Because of the way the Roman Catholic Church used James 5:14-16 to defend the Rite of Extreme Unction for centuries, Protestants have often been wary of anointing at all. Some have said that anointing was for apostolic times. They say that we no longer need such aids to faith, or that medical science has progressed beyond the need for such primitive measures. Other Protestants do practice anointing.[7]

8. Instead of swearing and grumbling, James has positive counsel for dealing with life patiently. Write down *what* he advises for each of the following circumstances, and *why* this is a wise course of action.

   if we are in trouble (5:13) _____

   _____

   _____

   _____

   _____

   _____

   if we are happy (5:13) _____

   _____

   _____

_____

_____

_____

if we are sick (5:14-18) _____

_____

_____

_____

_____

_____

_____

_____

9. Explain in your own words the two factors that heal a person in 5:15.

_____

_____

_____

_____

_____

_____

For Further Study:
a. When should we praise God (Psalm 34:1, Hebrews 13:15)?
    b. For what should we thank Him (Ephesians 5:20)?
    c. Why should we do these things?
    d. How can we thank Godeven for difficult circumstances?

For Further Study:
For more on question 8, especially reasons Scripture gives for prayer and praise, look at:
    a. Luke 11:5-13; James 1:5, 4:1-2; 1 John 5:14-15.
    b. Luke 17:11-19.

Healed (5:16). This Greek word refers to physical, psychological, and spiritual healing. To the Hebrews, mind, body, and spirit were all of one whole, and health was a unity (see Isaiah 53:5, Matthew 13:15, John 12:40). Thus, it is not clear whether James means that confession and prayer will lead to physical healing, spiritual healing (from sin), or both.

For Thought and Discussion: a. In your judgment, is it ever appropriate to confess sins before a group, such as an entire congregation? If so, under what circumstances? If not, why not?

b. Is it ever wise to confess personal sins to another person, even if that person is not directly involved? If so, when might it be appropriate, and why? If not, why not? What would be the neutral person's role in such a confession?

For Thought and Discussion: James seems to connect confession and forgiveness with healing (5:15-16). In your view, do confession and forgiveness contribute to physical as well as spiritual healing? Why or why not? (See, for example, 1 Corinthians 11:30.) Is sickness sometimes, never, or always due in part to unconfessed sin? Use Scripture as well as your experience to support your opinion.

10. Why is it so important to pray for each other's healing? (*Optional:* See Matthew 18:19-20, John 13:35, 1 Corinthians 12:12-26.)

_____

_____

_____

_____

_____

_____

11. What is the point of James's illustration about Elijah (James 5:17-18)?

_____

_____

_____

_____

_____

Love (5:19-20)

Hearing each other's confessions and praying for one another is part of being the family of God in the last days before Christ's return. Yet, if a brother's or sister's patience should fail and tempt him or her from the truth, we have a more active role also. We can't wait for the sinner to come to us for confession, for none of us faces trials and temptations alone.

Wander from the truth (5:19). There is some ambiguity in 5:19-20, but the point is clear. The wanderer is one of the **brothers**. This could mean a real believer or someone who belongs to the church and appears to be a believer (Acts 8:13-24, Hebrews 6:4-8, 2 Peter 2:20-21). The **death** (James 5:20) from which he is saved could be physical or spiritual death. Even if we believe that those whom God has saved are permanently saved, James wants us to be as concerned for the backsliding Christian as if we were not certain of his salvation (since we are in no position to judge whether his faith and salvation are genuine). No matter how we interpret 5:19-20, it is clear that a member of a Christian group has wandered from the truth of the gospel in both thought (*the truth*) and action (*his way*), and that he is in danger of some serious consequences.

12. Who in the church or fellowship has the responsibility to do something if a brother is seen to be wandering from the truth (5:19-20)?

_____

_____

_____

13. Only God can bring a sinner back and save him (John 6:44, Ephesians 1:7). So what does James mean by saying that one of us should bring the wanderer back and turn him from the error of his way?

_____

_____

_____

_____

_____

_____

_____

14. Explain in your own words the results of bringing back a wanderer (5:20), as you interpret them.

_____

_____

Optional Application: In light of 5:13-18, set aside time to pray about your needs, praise God for taking care of you, pray for someone, or confess your sins to someone.

For Thought and Discussion: What does James mean by saying that "The prayer of a *righteous* man is powerful and effective" (5:16)? Do we have to be sinless before God will answer our prayers? What does "righteous" mean? Consider: Was Elijah sinless (5:17)?

For Further Study: On Elijah, see 1 Kings 17:1-18:46.

For Thought and Discussion: What are some practical steps a person can take when he sees a brother wandering from the truth? Draw on Scripture and your own experience.

For Further Study: Add 5:7-20 to your outline.

_____

_____

_____

_____

_____

Your response

15. What one truth from 5:7-20 seems most significant to you?

_____

_____

_____

_____

_____

16. How can you apply this truth to your life this week?

_____

_____

_____

_____

_____

_____

17. List any questions you have about 5:7-20.

_____

_____

_____

_____

For the group

Warm-up. Question 2 would make a good warm-up.
You might want to ask first, "What is patience, in
the biblical sense?" We tend to use the English
word more for waiting without anxiety than for
enduring affliction without vengefulness or despair.

Read aloud and summarize.

Questions. When you understand what James means
by patience, examine his positive (the farmer, the
prophets) and negative (grumbling, swearing)
examples of patience. Then discuss some specific
areas of your lives in which you need to have
patience, and how you can act with patience in
those areas.

Prayer and praise (5:13) probably won't raise
any arguments, but anointing the sick (5:14-15)
may. Some members of your group may come from
Roman Catholic backgrounds where a particular
interpretation of these verses was taught, others
may come from Protestant backgrounds that decried
the Roman Catholic doctrine, and still others may
feel strongly for or against having non-clergy anoint
people for healing. Help the group examine what
the text actually says. Then discuss various ways in
which it might be applied today, or reasons why it is
no longer applicable. Support your views with careful reasoning.

Confessing your sins to each other (5:16) may
raise similar problems. Many people feel they have
received great benefit from confessing their sins to
clergy. However, many others regard the Roman
Catholic approach (required periodic confession to a
priest) as a travesty, and therefore altogether mis-
trust confession to anyone but God. Some Protestant churches practice public confession because of
James 5:16, while others point to the abuses (gossip, exhibitionism, titillation) public confession can
produce. Some Christians believe that the small
group (such as a Bible study group) is a good place
for confession, provided that all the members have
promised to keep private anything revealed in the
group. Other believers prefer to rely on spouses or
special friends for confession and prayer. J. A.
Motyer suggests that confession to fellow Christians
can be helpful if a) the person listening is doing so

with the "deliberate and single-minded intention to make it a matter of prayer. Only thus will we be delivered from the spirit of prying curiosity which, far from helping the needy out of his sin, would make the whole thing a matter of sin to the listener"; and b) the person confessing is doing so in order "to be healed, to be rid of that sin," not to shock or impress the hearer.[8] In short, both parties must examine their motives. You might consider Motyer's criteria if you discuss the merits of confessing to fellow believers. Examine both the potential benefits of sharing your sin-burdens with others and the potential dangers.

Your interpretation of 5:19-20 will depend partly on what you believe about "eternal security"—that is, if a person has ever truly believed in Jesus and been reborn, then is it possible for him to fall away from salvation? If you believe this is impossible, then either the wanderer is not a true believer or the death he risks is not eternal. However, James is, as usual, less concerned to teach about doctrine (such as eternal security) than about practice (what we should do when we are in no position to judge the genuineness of someone's faith and salvation). Discuss ways in which you can apply James's teaching without judging whether a person is "really saved." This teaching is extremely relevant, since it is so common to see fellow Christians in sin.

If you've spent much time on any of these knotty issues, you may find little time left to share what specific steps you each plan to take to apply something in 5:7-20. Try to plan ahead to allow time for this.

Worship. Thank God for promising that Christ's return is at hand, that the Judge is standing at the door. Thank Him for the prophets' examples of perseverance and patience. Praise Him for being full of compassion and mercy. Thank God also for promising to hear and answer prayers made in faith by righteous people. Thank Him for His eagerness to heal and forgive. Thank Him for your fellow believers who support you in prayer.

If you think it is appropriate in your group, take time all together or in pairs to confess any sins that are weighing on you. Pray for anyone who confesses, that they may be strengthened to resist that

108

sin from now on. Assure each other that those sins are completely forgiven (1 John 1:9). If you prefer, you can suggest that anyone who wants to share a burden can arrange a meeting later in private.

1. Tasker, pages 116-117.
2. Tasker, pages 117-118.
3. *The NIV Study Bible*, page 1885.
4. Tasker, pages 122-123.
5. Tasker, page 123.
6. *Rite of Anointing and Pastoral Care of the Sick* (New York: Pueblo, 1974), page 26. See also Barbara Leahy Shlemon, Dennis Linn, and Matthew Linn, *To Heal As Jesus Healed* (Notre Dame, Indiana: Ave Maria Press, 1978), pages 15, 18-23, 93-103.
7. For various views on anointing, see Motyer, pages 113-119; Tasker, pages 128-133; Davids, pages 193-194.
8. Motyer, pages 119-120.

REVIEW

After studying a book in detail for several weeks, it is helpful to examine the book as a whole again. A review can enable you to see how each individual topic contributes to the overall point the author wants to make. It can also help you trace themes and related ideas from chapter to chapter.

This review is fairly thorough. Feel free to take extra time to complete it or to omit some sections.

Teaching

1. First, reread all of James's letter. It should be familiar so you can read quickly, looking for threads that tie the book together. Pray for a fresh perspective on what God is saying.

2. James bases many of his practical exhortations on the nature of God. Write down what James says about God in each of the following passages, and describe at least one implication each statement has for our lives.

God's nature	implication
1:5	

God's nature	implication
1:13	
1:17	
1:20	
1:27	
2:5	
4:6	

God's nature	implication
4:12	
5:11	

3. Likewise, James also bases his teaching on the nature of man. What does he say about human beings in the following verses, and what are some implications for us?

Human nature	implications
1:18	
3:9	
4:14	

4. Summarize James's teaching on these topics:

trials (1:2-12, 5:7-16) _____

_____

_____

_____

_____

_____

_____

_____

temptations (1:13-18, 4:1-12, 5:19-20)

_____

_____

_____

_____

_____

_____

prayer (1:5-8, 4:1-3, 5:13-18) _____

_____

_____

_____

_____

_____

_____

the tongue (3:1-12; 4:1-3,11-12; 5:9,12)

_____

wisdom (1:5-8, 3:13-18) _____

wealth and poverty (1:9-11,27; 2:1-9; 5:1-6)

faith and deeds (1:22-27, 2:14-26, 3:13)

For Further Study:
If you have not been
making an outline of
James as you went
along, consider mak-
ing one now.

_____

_____

_____

single-mindedness and double-mindedness
(1:5-8,14,22-24; 2:4; 3:9-12,16-18; 4:1-10; 5:12)

_____

_____

_____

_____

_____

_____

_____

other major topics _____

_____

_____

_____

_____

_____

_____

5. In question 6 of lesson one (page 16), you said
   what you thought James's overall message or
   goal was. After studying the letter more thoroughly, how would you now summarize James's
   message?

_____

_____

_____

116

_____

_____

_____

6. Review the questions you listed at the ends of
   lessons one through eleven. Do any important
   ones remain unanswered? If so, some of the
   sources on pages 121-125 may help you answer
   some of them. You might also study some particular passage again on your own, or ask a
   mature believer.

Application

Having reviewed what James says, it is a good idea
to review how well you are doing it. Let this self-
examination be for confession, encouragement, and
growth, not for self-condemnation. Warren Wiersbe[1]
offers these questions to evaluate yourself:

- Am I becoming more and more patient in
  the testings of life?
- Do I play with temptation or resist it from
  the start?
- Do I find joy in obeying the Word of God, or
  do I merely study it and learn it?
- Are there any prejudices that shackle me?
- Am I able to control my tongue?
- Am I a peacemaker rather than a trouble-
  maker? Do people come to me for spiritual
  wisdom?
- Am I a friend of God or a friend of the world?
- Do I make plans without considering the
  will of God?
- Am I selfish when it comes to money? Am I
  unfaithful in the paying of my bills?
- Do I naturally depend on prayer when I find
  myself in some kind of trouble?
- Am I the kind of person others seek for
  prayer support?
- What is my attitude toward the wandering
  brother? Do I criticize and gossip, or do I
  seek to restore him in love?

7. Have you noticed any areas (thoughts, attitudes, behavior) in which you have changed as

a result of studying James? If so, how have you changed?

_____

_____

_____

_____

_____

_____

_____

8. Look back over the study at questions in which you planned some specific application. Are you satisfied with your follow-through? What areas continue to challenge you to further attention, and what do you plan to do about them?

_____

_____

_____

_____

_____

_____

_____

For the group

Read aloud. It might take fifteen minutes to read the whole letter of James aloud. You will probably find that this will refresh everyone's memory. However, if you prefer to save time, try reading just chapter 1.

Teaching. Unless you plan to take more than one meeting to cover this review, or unless your group is very adept at summarizing a book's teaching on a topic, you may want to select a few of the topics in

118

questions 2-4 for discussion. Choose those that you think are most important for your group to grasp. Then ask several people to tell how they would summarize James's message (question 5).

Let everyone ask his or her unanswered questions. Instead of allowing the group to rely on the leader for answers, suggest that various group members pursue answers in books or other sources. It is wise to begin training members to take as much responsibility as possible in the group. However, the leader should give whatever guidance is needed.

Application. Give everyone a chance to share answers to questions 7 and 8. You should know each other well enough by now to be specific. Hopefully, you have been sharing progress on application periodically and have been helping each other plan and follow through on applications. You have probably also been praying for each other. So, this should not be a time of boasting or despair, but of humility and mutual encouragement. You might apply James 5:16 together with regard to areas where you each need more growth.

Evaluation. Consider taking a few minutes or a whole meeting to evaluate how your group functioned during your study of James. Some questions you might ask are:

> How well did the study help you grasp the letter of James?
> What did you like best about your meetings?
> What did you like least? What would you change?
> How well did you meet the goals you set at your first meeting?
> What did you learn about small group study?
> What are members' current needs? What will you do next?

Worship. Thank God for what He has taught you and how He has been changing you through your study of James. Ask Him to continue to work on each of you in the areas you have named.

1. Warren W. Wiersbe, *Be Mature* (Wheaton, Illinois: Victor Books, 1978), page 176. We might add one question: Am I caring for the needy (1:27, 2:15-16)?

119

STUDY AIDS

For further information on the material in this study, consider the following sources. Your local Christian bookstore should be able to order any of them if it does not carry them. Most seminary libraries have them, as well as many university and public libraries.

Commentaries on James

Davids, Peter H. *The Epistle of James* (New International Greek Testament Commentary, Eerdmans, 1982).
    This is probably the best scholarly commentary on James currently available. However, Davids comments on the Greek text and is concerned with exegesis (explaining the meaning of each word, phrase, and passage) rather than application for today, so those who want English only and an emphasis on application might do better with another commentary.

Motyer, J. A. *The Tests of Faith* (InterVarsity Press, 1970).
    Motyer explains the text with an eye toward helping modern people apply it to themselves. This is excellent material for reflection and new insights into James's message.

Tasker, R. V. G. *The General Epistle of James* (Tyndale New Testament Commentary, Eerdmans, 1956).
    Eerdmans has recently replaced this volume of its Tyndale Series with a new one by James Moo. Both books are fine works that explain the text for the English reader and suggest some areas of application. Either one would be a good, inexpensive first commentary on James.

Wiersbe, Warren W. *Be Mature* (Victor Books, 1978).
    This exposition reads like good sermons on the book of James in

Wiersbe's inimitable style. Wiersbe uses many illustrations from his pastoral experience to help the reader apply James's teaching.

Historical and Background Sources

Bruce, F. F. *New Testament History* (Doubleday, 1979).
A readable history of Herodian kings, Roman governors, philosophical schools, Jewish sects, Jesus, the early Jerusalem church, Paul, and early gentile Christianity. Well-documented with footnotes for the serious student, but the notes do not intrude.

Harrison, E. F. *Introduction to the New Testament* (Eerdmans, 1971).
History from Alexander the Great—who made Greek culture dominant in the biblical world—through philosophies, pagan and Jewish religion, Jesus' ministry and teaching (the weakest section), and the spread of Christianity. Very good maps and photographs of the land, art, and architecture of New Testament times.

Packer, James I., Merrill C. Tenney, William White, Jr. *The Bible Almanac* (Thomas Nelson, 1980).
One of the most accessible handbooks of the people of the Bible and how they lived. Lots of photos and illustrations liven an already readable text.

Concordances, Dictionaries, and Handbooks

A *concordance* lists words of the Bible alphabetically along with each verse in which the word appears. It lets you do your own word studies. An *exhaustive* concordance lists every word used in a given translation, while an *abridged* or *complete* concordance omits either some words, some occurrences of the word, or both.

The two best exhaustive concordances are *Strong's Exhaustive Concordance* and *Young's Analytical Concordance to the Bible*. Both are available based on the King James Version of the Bible and the New American Standard Bible. *Strong's* has an index by which you can find out which Greek or Hebrew word is used in a given English verse. *Young's* breaks up each English word it translates. However, neither concordance requires knowledge of the original language.

Among other good, less expensive concordances, *Cruden's Complete Concordance* is keyed to the King James and Revised Versions, and *The NIV Complete Concordance* is keyed to the New International Version. These include all references to every word included, but they omit "minor" words. They also lack indexes to the original languages.

A ***Bible dictionary*** or ***Bible encyclopedia*** alphabetically lists articles about people, places, doctrines, important words, customs, and geography of the Bible.

The New Bible Dictionary, edited by J. D. Douglas, F. F. Bruce, J. I. Packer, N. Hillyer, D. Guthrie, A. R. Millard, and D. J. Wiseman (Tyndale, 1982) is more comprehensive than most dictionaries. Its 1300 pages include quantities of information along with excellent maps, charts, diagrams, and an index for cross-referencing.

Unger's Bible Dictionary by Merrill F. Unger (Moody, 1979) is equally good and is available in an inexpensive paperback edition.

The Zondervan Pictorial Encyclopedia edited by Merrill C. Tenney (Zondervan, 1975, 1976) is excellent and exhaustive, and is being revised and updated in the 1980's. However, its five 1000-page volumes are a financial investment, so all but very serious students may prefer to use it at a church, public, college, or seminary library.

Unlike a Bible dictionary in the above sense, *Vine's Expository Dictionary of New Testament Words* by W. E. Vine (various publishers) alphabetically lists major words used in the King James Version and defines each New Testament Greek word that KJV translates with that English word. *Vine's* lists verse references where that Greek word appears, so that you can do your own cross-references and word studies without knowing any Greek.

Vine's is a good basic book for beginners, but it is much less complete than other Greek helps for English speakers. More serious students might prefer *The New International Dictionary of New Testament Theology*, edited by Colin Brown (Zondervan) or *The Theological Dictionary of the New Testament* by Gerhard Kittel and Gerhard Friedrich, abridged in one volume by Geoffrey W. Bromiley (Eerdmans).

A *Bible atlas* can be a great aid to understanding what is going on in a book of the Bible and how geography affected events. Here are a few good choices:

The Macmillan Atlas by Yohanan Aharoni and Michael Avi-Yonah (Macmillan, 1968, 1977) contains 264 maps, 89 photos, and 12 graphics. The many maps of individual events portray battles, movements of people, and changing boundaries in detail.

The New Bible Atlas by J. J. Bimson and J. P. Kane (Tyndale, 1985) has 73 maps, 34 photos, and 34 graphics. Its evangelical perspective, concise and helpful text, and excellent research make it a very good choice, but its greatest strength is its outstanding graphics, such as cross-sections of the Dead Sea.

The Bible Mapbook by Simon Jenkins (Lion, 1984) is much shorter and less expensive than most other atlases, so it offers a good first taste of the usefulness of maps. It contains 91 simple maps, very little text, and 20 graphics. Some of the graphics are computer-generated and intriguing.

The Moody Atlas of Bible Lands by Barry J. Beitzel (Moody, 1984) is scholarly, very evangelical, and full of theological text, indexes, and references. This admirable reference work will be too deep and costly for some, but Beitzel shows vividly how God prepared the land of Israel perfectly for the acts of salvation He was going to accomplish in it.

A *handbook* of biblical customs can also be useful. Some good ones are *Today's Handbook of Bible Times and Customs* by William L. Coleman

(Bethany, 1984) and the less detailed *Daily Life in Bible Times* (Nelson, 1982).

For Small Group Leaders

The Small Group Leader's Handbook by Steve Barker et al. (InterVarsity, 1982).
　　Written by an InterVarsity small group with college students primarily in mind. It includes information on small group dynamics and how to lead in light of them, and many ideas for worship, building community, and outreach. It has a good chapter on doing inductive Bible study.

Getting Together: A Guide for Good Groups by Em Griffin (InterVarsity, 1982).
　　Applies to all kinds of groups, not just Bible studies. From his own experience, Griffin draws deep insights into why people join groups; how people relate to each other; and principles of leadership, decision making, and discussions. It is fun to read, but its 229 pages will take more time than the above book.

You Can Start a Bible Study Group by Gladys Hunt (Harold Shaw, 1984).
　　Builds on Hunt's thirty years of experience leading groups. This book is wonderfully focused on God's enabling. It is both clear and applicable for Bible study groups of all kinds.

How to Lead Small Groups by Neal F. McBride (NavPress, 1990).
　　Covers leadership skills for all kinds of small groups—Bible study, fellowship, task, and support groups. Filled with step-by-step guidance and practical exercises to help you grasp the critical aspects of small group leadership and dynamics.

The Small Group Letter, a special section in *Discipleship Journal* (NavPress).
　　Unique. Its four pages per issue, six issues per year are packed with practical ideas for small groups. It stays up to date because writers discuss what they are currently doing as small group members and leaders. To subscribe, write to Subscription Services, Post Office Box 54470, Boulder, Colorado 80323-4470.

Bible Study Methods

Braga, James. *How to Study the Bible* (Multnomah, 1982).
　　Clear chapters on a variety of approaches to Bible study: synthetic, geographical, cultural, historical, doctrinal, practical, and so on. Designed to help the ordinary person without seminary training to use these approaches.

Fee, Gordon, and Douglas Stuart. *How to Read the Bible For All Its Worth* (Zondervan, 1982).

After explaining in general what interpretation (exegesis) and application (hermeneutics) are, Fee and Stuart offer chapters on interpreting and applying the different kinds of writing in the Bible: Epistles, Gospels, Old Testament Law, Old Testament narrative, the Prophets, Psalms, Wisdom, and Revelation. Fee and Stuart also suggest good commentaries on each biblical book. They write as evangelical scholars who personally recognize Scripture as God's Word for their daily lives.

Jensen, Irving L. *Independent Bible Study* (Moody, 1963), and *Enjoy Your Bible* (Moody, 1962).

The former is a comprehensive introduction to the inductive Bible study method, especially the use of synthetic charts. The latter is a simpler introduction to the subject.

Wald, Oletta. *The Joy of Discovery in Bible Study* (Augsburg, 1975).

Wald focuses on issues such as how to observe all that is in a text, how to ask questions of a text, how to use grammar and passage structure to see the writer's point, and so on. Very helpful on these subjects.

Other titles in the *Lifechange* series you may be interested in: